Walk!
Tenerife South

David Brawn
Ros Brawn

DISCOVERY WALKING GUIDES LTD

Walk! Tenerife South

First published - February 2003
Copyright © 2003

Published by
Discovery Walking Guides Ltd
10 Tennyson Close, Northampton NN5 7HJ,
England

Maps
Maps are adapted from **Tenerife Walkers' Maps**
published by **Discovery Walking Guides Ltd**

Photographs
All photographs in this book were taken by the
authors, David Brawn and Ros Brawn.

Front Cover Photograph
Looking north from the top of Roque del Conde
(Walk 14)

Rear Cover Photographs
Top: Taken on Walk 10, 'Wow! Spectacular'.
Centre: Near the start of 'Queen Of The South',
Walk 11
Bottom: 'Coastal Escapism', Walk 5.

ISBN 1-899554-11-4

Text, maps and photographs © David & Ros
Brawn 2003

Walk! Tenerife South

Contents

David & Ros Brawn

David and Ros have lived and worked in England, Papua New Guinea and the Seychelles before settling for a number of years in Tenerife. David's first published books were accountancy texts.

David and Ros have been walking and writing for Discovery Walking Guides since it began, researching guides for most of the Canary Islands, the Balearic Islands, Malta, Gozo, Madeira, and the Alpujarras. More recently they have surveyed and mapped a number of these regions using satellite navigation equipment combined with cartographic software.

Considering themselves as semi-permanent travellers, they divide their non-research time between Spain and Northampton, England.

David is a member of the British Cartographic Society.

FOREWORD

It all started as a little walk designed to promote the BookSwop. Called 'Geranium Walk', it started in Los Cristianos and wound its way along the coastal promenade all the way to what was then the far end of Playa de las Américas at Puerto Colón Marina and the BookSwop. That was in 1988, and so popular did this route become that the authorities have officially named the promenade 'Geranium Walk'.

Discovery Walking Guides began as a series of occasional walks in BookSwop newsletters. From these humble beginnings it was soon clear that people wanted more, and the first two 'Warm Island Walking Guides', Tenerife North and Tenerife South, were published, including painstakingly hand-drawn maps.

Being resident in Tenerife, it was logical for us to expand the WIWG titles to include other Canary Islands. 'OS' equivalent map sections were licenced from the Spanish authorities, at a cost, releasing time for research though the maps were often out of date and needed correction by DWG. New titles were added steadily, including publications for La Gomera, Gran Canaria, Lanzarote, El Hierro and La Palma. Inevitably, destinations further afield joined the stable; Mallorca, Ibiza and Menorca in the Balearic Islands, Malta and Gozo, Madeira, The Alpujarras; and the first outside walking authors were taken on to research and write guides for the Algarve. Since then, authors for the new Alpujarras and Lanzarote titles have joined DWG. The format of the walking guides has developed from simple folded maps and walking descriptions, to the current book format that you are now reading, and the '34 Walks' Series.

Cartography
As the company expanded, it became more obvious that the quality of existing maps left a lot to be desired. The answer was clear - DWG would become cartographers, taking on the research and mapping of the walking areas. This steep learning curve was made easier by the miracle of surveying systems based on satellite navigation technology and the new cartographic software. Combine these with the vast increases in portable computer power and you have the mobile ground survey systems that we use today.

The map data collected was not only ideal for enhancing walking guides; the new maps were in demand as publications in their own right, and so 'Tour & Trail Maps' were launched. Since then, 'Drive! Maps' have joined the publication lists, and more recently maps printed on virtually indestructible materials, including titles published by The Indestructible Map Company.

Research
All the walking routes contained in this book have been walked by the authors and are recorded on our mobile ground survey system. Edited versions of the ground survey, taking out the getting lost/false trails/routes which didn't work out, are available as Personal Navigator Files for GPS users with compatible GPS software. We really can prove exactly where our research has taken us, unlike some walking publications we come across. All DWG authors are now required to compile their routes using our mobile ground survey system, guaranteeing that all routes have been walked by the author.

Feedback
When new editions are prepared, it is with the assistance of input by many of the users of DWG's maps and guides. No matter how carefully prepared a publication may be, as soon as it is published some changes inevitably take place - a dirt track is sealed with tarmac, a bar changes its name, a walk is re-routed because of landslip or new fences. Feedback from users can be added to newsletters and DWG websites, until new editions are published which incorporate the updates.

Write to:-

DWG Ltd.
10 Tennyson Close
Northampton NN5 7HJ
England

David & Ros Brawn

MAP NOTES

The map sections used in **Walk! Tenerife South** are greyscale versions adapted from **Tenerife Walkers' Maps** published by Discovery Walking Guides Ltd. In the interests of clarity, not all waypoints referred to in the walk descriptions are shown on the map sections.

Tenerife Walkers' Maps contain 1:25,000 full colour topographical maps covering all the regions explored by **34 Tenerife Walks** (including Walk! Tenerife South), and are available in conventional paper and super-durable (waterproof and tear-proof) editions. For more information on DWG publications write to Discovery Walking Guides Ltd, 10 Tennyson Close, Northampton NN5 7HJ, England or visit:

www.walking.demon.co.uk and **www.dwgwalking.co.uk**

Map Legend

Roads, tracks and trails

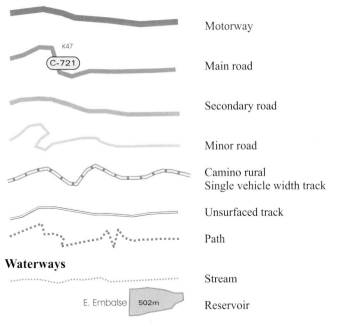

	Motorway
	Main road
	Secondary road
	Minor road
	Camino rural / Single vehicle width track
	Unsurfaced track
	Path

Waterways

	Stream
E. Embalse 502m	Reservoir

General features

𝄪 Lighthouse	≪ Mirador, viewpoint	◊ Spring
⌂ Tower	ℹ Information	⛽ Petrol
⚲ Ermita, chapel	⌂ Hotel	⚏ Bar/Restaurant
⊡ Football, sports ground	⚿ Picnic area	⊕ GPS Waypoint
⚑ Church	⊞ Cemetery	

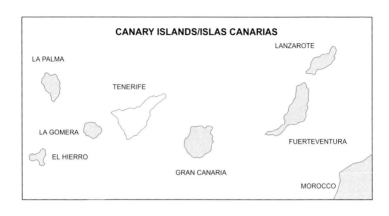

CANARY ISLANDS/ISLAS CANARIAS

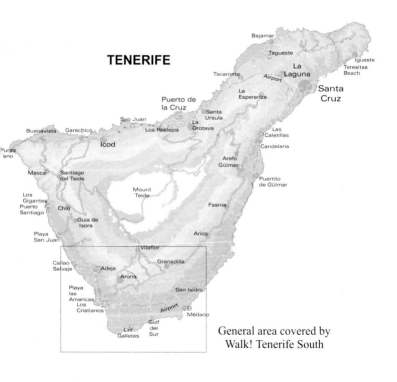

TENERIFE

General area covered by Walk! Tenerife South

WALKS LOCATOR MAP

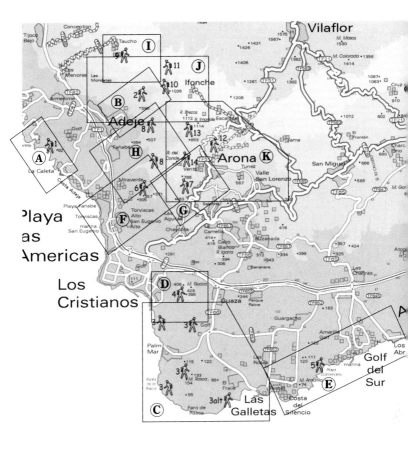

Ⓐ	Walk 1	Life In The Raw	
Ⓑ	Walk 2	Barranco del Infierno	
Ⓒ	Walk 3	Barren Grandeur	
Ⓓ	Walk 4	Mount Guaza	
Ⓔ	Walk 5	Coastal Escapism	
Ⓕ	Walk 6	Picos Las Américas	

Ⓖ	Walk 7	Down To Town
Ⓗ	Walk 8	Adeje Skywalker
Ⓘ	Walk 9	Taucho Tour
Ⓙ	Walk 10	Wow! Spectacular
	Walk 11	Queen Of The South
Ⓚ	Walk 12	Walkers Who Lunch
	Walk 13	Fantasia
	Walk 14	Table Mountain

NAVIGATION AND GPS

Walk! Tenerife South routes include GPS Waypoints. These refer to specific points along each walking route. A full GPS Waypoint list is provided for each walking route, although not all waypoints are shown on the maps. To use these GPS Waypoints, remember to set your **GPS datum** to **Pico las Nieves**; this datum may be referred to as Canary Islands or Islas Canarias on some GPS receivers. Using the wrong datum can result in significant errors in location.

GPS Waypoints are given in **Latitude/Longitude** coordinates; e.g. start of Barranco del Infierno behind Otello's Bar is Wp.1 28 07.491 N (Latitude) and 16 43.316 W (Longitude). When inputting the Waypoints to your GPS, do remember to have your GPS set to Pico las Nieves datum.

GPS Waypoints are approximate positions, and while we quote positions to 0.001 minutes of arc (approximately 1 metre accuracy) in practice 0.010 minutes of arc (10 metres) is an acceptable standard of accuracy. Note that on the map sections for each walk the GPS Waypoint symbol is placed alongside the walking route for clarity, not on the exact location to which it refers.

Waypoints alone are no substitute for an accurately written walk description, but will ensure that you know when you reach particular points in the walk description and that you are heading in approximately the right direction. Discovery Walking Guides are developing 'Personal Navigator Files' for all their new walking guide books, providing full GPS track and waypoint information for each walking route. These 'Personal Navigator Files' can be downloaded to your GPS receiver, via GPS software, so that you walk in the same footsteps as the author of the guide book. More information on 'Personal Navigator Files' is available on DWG's websites:

www.walking.demon.co.uk and **www.dwgwalking.co.uk**

SYMBOLS RATING GUIDE

- our rating for effort/exertion:
1 very easy   **2** easy
3 average   **4** energetic
5 strenuous

- approximate time to complete the walk (compare your times against ours early in a walk)

- approximate walking distance in kms

- approximate ascents/descents in metres

- from **0** (none available), up to **5** (exceptional food/drink/position)

THE SHAPING OF TENERIFE SOUTH

From Agriculture To Tourism

Before tourism became its most important industry, much of the south of Tenerife was a patchwork of plantations and *fincas*. The hotels and apartments of the resorts stand on land once painstakingly terraced, producing a variety of crops including bananas, tomatoes and grapes. Terrace walls hand-built from rock, stones and boulders served a dual purpose; they made the steep volcanic slopes more workable, and they helped prevent the erosion of precious top soil.

Then there was the problem of irrigation to solve. It might seem at first glance that the island, especially the south, must be seriously short of water, but though the rainfall on the coastal areas is low there is plenty of precipitation at higher altitudes. The farmers therefore built a network of water channels to run across the surface of the land.

From the 1960s, tourism began to take on importance in the south, and its growth has continued steadily. For all the criticism that is sometimes levelled at this rapid expansion, tourism has provided many much-needed jobs and has, on balance, been good for the island. But one result has been the loss of agriculture. Although commercial scale banana plantations are still found in the south, the attractions of a job in tourism leave the hard life of wresting a living from the land a poor second choice for many Canarians.

The remnants of terracing are still visible on the slopes, and sections of the irrigation system remain. A few still carry water. Even where the original open canals are disused, modern pipe work often runs alongside these old systems, confirming that these old waterways were built along the most logical routes. You will see many examples of terracing and water canals on a number of walks in this book, often in seemingly inaccessible places.

Plant Life

Even the *malpais* areas of the south, which seem to consist of rough, naked lava rock, support plant life. The area covered by the walks in this book takes in a wide variety of species, from the desert plants adapted to harsh, hot almost soil-free areas, to the pine forests. The *barrancos* explored on our walks are often filled with lush flowering plants, many unique to Tenerife (for example,

Photo opportunity - Roque del Conde in the background, ancient and modern water systems in the foreground providing moisture for lush plant life including *Lavandula canariensis*. (Walk 13, Fantasia)

Walk 2, 'Barranco del Infierno'), and the phenomenon of the bramble-choked *barranco* seen on **Walk 9, 'Taucho Tour'** is, in our experience, unique. The mountain slopes which face the moist onshore winds are studded

Common in Tenerife, the cardón or Candelabra Cactus(*Euphorbia canariensis*).

with strange, endemic succulents, while ancient almond trees, olives, Canarian palms and figs have established themselves in the more fertile pockets.

As for cultivated plant life; you will see grape vines, potatoes, tomatoes, oranges, lemons, avocados and papaya growing in village gardens, and many ornamental plants including hibiscus and bougainvillea (for example, **Walk 12, 'Walkers Who Lunch'**) and on the fertile upland fields in the Ifonche area (**Walk 10, 'Wow! Spectacular'** and **Walk 11, 'Queen Of The South'**).

*For the enthusiast, a 'bible' of flowering plants of the Canary Islands 'Flores Silvestres de Las Islas Canarias', (authors David and Zoé Bramwell, published by Editorial Rueda of Madrid, ISBN 84-7207-062-X) provides the most comprehensive information, although this is not always available in English translation. 'Native Flora of the Canary Islands' (author M A C Pérez, published by Everest, ISBN 84-241-3555-5) is less detailed but in English.

Wildlife

Wild rabbits thrive on Tenerife, and you may see wild goats while following our walks, while a few *cabreros* still tend herds of goats, even as close to mass tourism as Mount Guaza and the Guaza Plateau, on **Walk 3, 'Barren Grandeur'** or **Walk 4, 'Mount Guaza'**. Bird lovers will have more to watch out for although these are more often heard than seen, with the exception of birds of prey which cruise the slopes and the *hoopoe* with its distinctive black and white wings. Various species of gulls and sea birds will accompany you on coastal routes such as **Walk 5, 'Coastal Escapism'**, or **Walk 1, 'Life In The Raw'**. Lizards of various species are easier to spot, as are butterflies in sizes from thumbnail to hand-sized. Other insect life that you are likely to spot while walking includes several species of bees, dragonflies, moths, beetles (look out for the cochineal beetles in their protective coating of white dust which colonise prickly pear cacti), and spiders.

You rarely see two goats with similar colouring.

*A weighty tome, in Spanish but liberally illustrated, is 'Naturaleza de las Islas Canarias' (published by Turquesa, ISBN 84-95412-18-17) should satisfy the keenest wildlife specialist.

*For these titles and other Canary Islands books and maps try Libreria Barbara, Calle General Franco, 38650 Los Cristianos, Tel/Fax: 922 792301 (PO Box 216, 38650 Los Cristianos)

SAFETY

Safety is all about how you walk, and what you take with you. Start with suitable equipment, especially footwear (comfortable, good grip, tough) and sun protection (high factor cream, hat). Dangerous situations can arise through :-

- **Lack of concentration**; always 'Look where you are stepping, and STOP to look at the view'.
- **Tiredness**; walk within your physical limit, and when on strenuous routes, stop and rest whenever you feel the need to recover. This is *not* a race.
- **Sunburn/sunstroke**; wear suitable clothing, hat and sunglasses and high factor sun cream. You can walk in the sun, but always try to rest in the shade.
- **Dehydration**; drink lots of water before, during and after walking.
- **Keep to the route**; even experienced walkers can get lost in unfamiliar terrain.
- **Keep others informed**; let someone responsible know where you are going.
- **If the route ahead is impassable, or if bad weather sets in**; turn back and retrace your steps to the start point.

WHAT TO TAKE

We suggest you take a daypack on any walk. Here's our basic packing list:-

guide book/map

GPS and/or **compass**

2 x ½ litre bottles water per person

snack

lightweight waterproof **jacket**

hat (functional, not Ascot)

sunglasses

plasters

antiseptic cream or wipes

tweezers (for cactus spines)

whistle

camera

secateurs (for overgrown routes)

money (folding and change)

taxi phone numbers

mobile phone

bus timetable

WEATHER FOR WALKERS

Tenerife's pleasant climate is one of the main reasons that its tourism industry is so successful. It is unusual for the temperature to drop below 16°C in the winter - if you can call it that - or much above 32°C in midsummer (July to mid-September). From the walker's point of view, these summer months are not ideal for tackling anything but short, undemanding walks with plenty of shade along the route.

From September onwards, the temperatures begin to ease and become ideal for walking, although the sun is still strong and must be treated with respect. Always remember to protect yourself from the sun, and to take (and drink) plenty of water, whenever you walk. The climate remains good for walking from around September up until June (approximately), with few exceptions.

When the rains come to the south of Tenerife, they can be dramatic. For most of the year you can almost guarantee that rain will not fall, but from November to February there can be the occasional powerful electrical storm, accompanied by torrential downpours that always catch the authorities unawares (the Canarian version of 'leaves on the line'). If you are planning a winter walk in Tenerife south and the skies are leaden and the winds blustery, especially from the south-west or north-west, it may well be best to postpone your plans. But even in winter, you would have to be unlucky to experience more than two or three consecutive wild, wet days. Do bear in mind that walking routes may be disrupted after severe weather. Even when you have started out on a perfect day, be aware that the weather on any island, and particularly if you are walking at altitude, is liable to rapid change. Be prepared to abandon your walk and retrace your steps if bad weather threatens.

A few times each year, the island is affected by an unpleasant *sirocco* wind (locally also called *calima*) from Africa; it is hot and laden with Saharan sand and dust which slowly falls and gets everywhere. The temperature rises and stays high, and visibility is reduced. It would be foolish to choose to inhale any more of this air than is necessary, so it is best to avoid walking at these times.

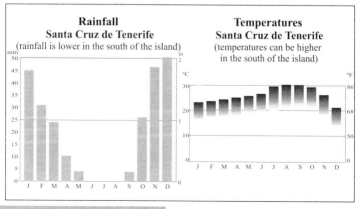

Rainfall
Santa Cruz de Tenerife
(rainfall is lower in the south of the island)

Temperatures
Santa Cruz de Tenerife
(temperatures can be higher
in the south of the island)

1. LIFE IN THE RAW

This walk leaves tourism behind and heads off into countryside, providing an excellent introduction to the rugged southern landscapes. Our route begins in **La Caleta** and follows coastal paths, taking in the hippie colony at **Spaghetti Beach**, beaches and *barrancos* before reaching our half way point at **El Puertito**, where we take a break, then returning with variations to our start point.

Our start point is in the village of **La Caleta**, just inland from the sea at the cross roads on **Calle Las Artes** where we head west (**Wp.1, W**) on the new road and past a roundabout, then going right onto a dirt road before taking the steep rock path up the ridge, the stone drumming from our footfalls, aiming for the signboard visible on the ridge. We reach the ridge (**Wp.2, 6M**) and step through a low stone wall, passing two *Espacio Naturaleza Protegido* signs, our manicured dirt path running ahead, other paths running left and right from the signs. At another junction of paths running seawards and inland (**Wp.3, 8M**), we have a choice of routes into **Hippie Valley**; ahead is the steeper route, while we take the right hand option marked as suitable for wheelchairs!

Once named Spaghetti Beach in the days when an Italian naturist chef cooked here, wearing only a sea captain's cap, this 'alternative' valley is dotted with hippie shacks of rock boulders and palm fronds, and tepees. The path runs around the valley giving us an arms' length view of the natural lifestyle, crossing the valley's watercourse (**Wp.4, 10M**), on a stone-laid section before it runs gently down to meet the shorter route (**Wp.5, 13M**).

Our path climbs gently before starting a steep ascent of the valley's western wall. Just before the top of our climb (**Wp.6, 18M**), a path goes left as we continue up to a marker post at a junction of paths (**Wp.7**). Continuing ahead, we cross the high ground and begin dropping down into *barranco* country, waves breaking far below us as we descend on the well-made trail to more hippie encampments in the *barranco*. This large cove is formed by three *barrancos* meeting the sea, giving rise to interesting geological formations.

We cross the *barranco* watercourse (**Wp.8, 23M**) and climb gently uphill, staying on the main path and ignoring side paths off to camping areas. Over the headland between the two *barrancos* by a blue tepee (**Wp.9, 27M**), our path is now stone over rock, heading towards long-abandoned plantations on the far side of the second *barranco*. We begin to drop into the second *barranco* (**Wp.10**), the path much less clear now until it crosses the watercourse (**Wp.11, 31M**). As we ascend we come onto a clearer path which meanders along to the remains of an old dirt road, becoming concrete as it climbs (**Wp.12**) towards an abandoned plantation. The concrete comes to an end (**Wp.13, 34M**) and we drop into another small *barranco* before climbing rock sheets to come up to a dirt road around the old plantation (**Wp.14, 36M**). We follow the dirt road inland, running up into the valley past abandoned

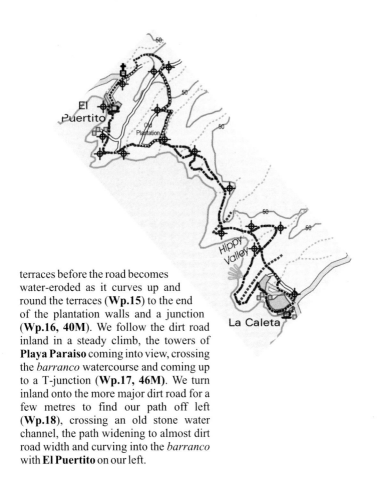

terraces before the road becomes
water-eroded as it curves up and
round the terraces (**Wp.15**) to the end
of the plantation walls and a junction
(**Wp.16, 40M**). We follow the dirt road
inland in a steady climb, the towers of
Playa Paraiso coming into view, crossing
the *barranco* watercourse and coming up
to a T-junction (**Wp.17, 46M**). We turn
inland onto the more major dirt road for a
few metres to find our path off left
(**Wp.18**), crossing an old stone water
channel, the path widening to almost dirt
road width and curving into the *barranco*
with **El Puertito** on our left.

The path swings left to an electricity pylon (**Wp.19**) and a path runs along the
spur of bare rock before becoming indistinct. We continue down the spur to
lose height before we need to leave the ridge and scramble down the rocks and
stone slopes (**Wp.20**) to meet an old dirt road at the back of the village
(**Wp.21, 57M**) which takes us to **El Puertito's** small church and parking area
(**Wp.22**), to step onto the tarmac road curving down to the sea front of **El
Puertito** and **Pepe y Lola's** little bar (**Wp.23, 63M**).

After refreshment we begin our return (**0M**) by walking in front of the bar and
following the path which wriggles between the jumble of houses to climb out
of the bay and onto a headland where we pick up the coastal path. We cross a
dirt road (**Wp.24, 5M**) and continue on the coastal route, passing another
Espacio Natureleza Protegido signpost with no board (**Wp.25**) as we head
towards the old plantation that we skirted on the outward route.

Our route widens to a dirt road taking us to the edge of the *barranco* (**Wp.26**)
and onto a path which descends to its floor, crossing it on an old stone wall and
climbing up towards the banana plantation on the next headland, heading
towards its nearest corner where rock steps take us up to the level of the

plantation and a dirt road.

Following the dirt road right, we meet our outward route (**Wp.14**) and retrace our steps across the *barranco* before descending the concrete and dirt road. This time we walk along the pebble foreshore to climb/scramble up onto the headland. Before reaching our outward route (at **Wp.9**) we take a path above the sea, waves crashing on interesting rock formations, before dropping down to the sea and its 'cossie-optional' beach suitable for bathing.

Climbing away from the 'beach', our path wriggles up the slopes to join our main path (our outward route, **Wp.27, 26M**). We retrace our route down the steep path into **Hippie Valley** but this time we take the short route across the valley (**Wp.5**). After the valley's impressive watercourse, we face a steep climb up the eastern wall, back to the junction of paths (**Wp.3**).

This time we turn right for an easy stroll seawards with dramatic views over **Hippie Valley** and its cove, the views becoming even more impressive as our path comes to the cliff edge (take care) before the route swings left (**Wp.28**) We come to a low stone wall (**Wp.29**) where a path goes left to **Wp.2**. Through the wall, our path runs inland to the rear of new apartments (**Wp.30**). You could take a quick route back to our start point, but we turn right to drop down the wide stairs to ground level, where we go right to the second bay of **La Caleta**. A path leads through the houses to the sea front bar, from where we head up the narrow road past a fish restaurant on our right to the crossroads at our start point.

2. BARRANCO DEL INFIERNO

Behind the county town of **Adeje** is Tenerife's most popular walk - the **Barranco del Infierno**. Local legend says the gorge is so deep the sun never reaches the bottom, and while this is unlikely to be true the 'barranco architecture' of the walk should not be missed. Easy access by bus (416, 441 or 473) from **Los Cristianos** and **Playa de las Américas**. This walk is extremely popular so we advise an early start and avoid weekends.

Taking the bus from the resort, ask for **Barranco del Infierno**, and get off at the highest stop in **Adeje**; the town's expansion now means that you will have a bit of an uphill walk past the Town Hall (*Ayuntamiento*) and church to go left to the cannon outside **Villa de Adeje** and follow the road round to the right. A very steep climb takes you up to **Otello's** (closed Tuesdays) and the walk starts directly behind the restaurant (**Wp.1, 0M**). Car parking can be a problem close to **Otello's** and you may have to park at the bottom of the steep hill.

After that steep climb to the official start of Tenerife's most 'manicured' and popular walk, you can rest up on the shaded seating before setting off down the stone-laid track behind **Otello's**. The trail clings to the northern face of the *barranco* for the first half of our journey (**30-45M**). Although the path has been levelled and edged, with stairs for ascents and descents, it is still an energetic walk. Our route hugs the cliff face and so has excellent views, though the precipitous drops at the edge of the path might disturb vertigo sufferers. There are several turns with viewing points along this first section for those essential photographs, or for just taking a breather; (**Wp.2, 9M**) viewing platform, (**Wp.3**) crossing the watercourse in the side **Barranco Chavon**, (**Wp.4, 15M**) spectacularly sited viewing platform, (**Wp.5**) cross working canal on small bridge, (**Wps.6 & 7**) viewing platforms.

Just about the time you're thinking this is a 'nice' walk with great views but are wondering why people say it is 'spectacular', the trail leads down into the *barranco*. We drop down to cross the water canal on another log bridge (**Wp.8**) and come down to a wooden bridge over the *barranco*'s watercourse (**Wp.9, 33M**). From here the nature of our walk changes as we follow the stream along the floor of the canyon. Now we are in close contact with the plants of Tenerife, but please do not pick flowers or uproot plants as this is a protected area.

Reaching **La Cojedra** (**Wp.10, 39M** and well signed), you may think that this cliff face represents the famous waterfall, but the water pipes leading along the path show there is still some way to go. **La Cojedra** makes a pleasant resting point before tackling the final stage. A water canal tumbles invitingly past, providing cool relief for hot faces and limbs.

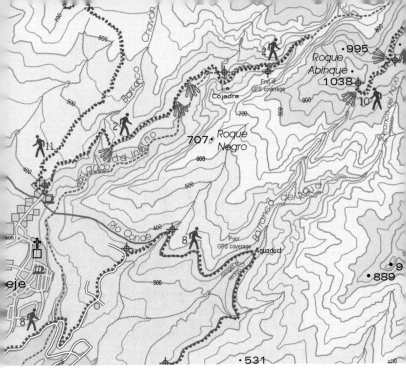

The path after **La Cojedra** is hemmed in by bushes, while cliffs close over us as we criss-cross the stream on bridges (**Wps.11, 12 and 13**); after which we lose any GPS signal due to the sheer-sided *barranco*. As we progress the 'Barranco Architecture' becomes increasingly spectacular, with the path leading us alongside the stream, and criss-crossing it, beneath the towering heights. Only at the very end does the path peter out leaving us with a scramble over rocks before turning the last corner. Hidden until the last few metres of the walk, the waterfall is very impressive as it cascades 100 metres down the sheer face of the *barranco* into a still pool. For this sight alone the **Barranco del Infierno** should be included in everyone's itinerary of Southern Tenerife.

There is no way up and over the *barranco,* so we return by retracing our steps, including the stiff climb up from the *barranco* floor.

Otello's (closed Tuesdays) at the end of the walk is the logical, and nearest, place for refreshment. Sitting in the restaurant you can enjoy the view down over **Adeje** to the coast, or a view up into the *barranco* from their rear terrace, while tucking into the local speciality - Garlic Chicken (Pollo al Ajillo). **Adeje** has several good value bar/restaurants including **Oasis** and **La Rambla** below the town hall with another couple of *tipicos* across the road. Garlic chicken is the local speciality and is available in most bar/restaurants.

As **Barranco del Infierno** is the most popular walk in Tenerife, it is best to begin early if you want to avoid the crowds. A 9.30 start gives the best conditions, avoids most of the crowds, and you can finish the walk with lunch.

3. BARREN GRANDEUR

Deserts and deserted coastlines have a beauty all their own. Here we tour the 'Barren Grandeur' of the **Guaza Plateau** and deserted coastline out to **Faro de Rasca** lighthouse, returning by an inland route. From the lighthouse we also have an alternative route to finish in **Las Galletas**, with its frequent bus service back to **Los Cristianos**. Starting from the southern end of **Los Cristianos** we are immediately into the desert, with very limited refreshment opportunities, which assumes its own beauty when seen at close quarters.

3 | 3.75 hours | 14.7 km | 200m / 200m | 0

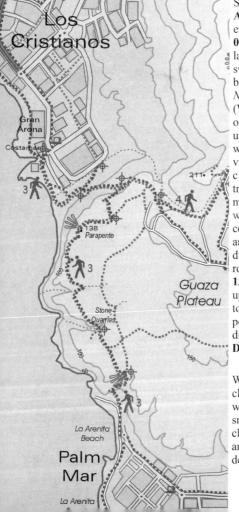

Starting from the **Costamar Apartments** at the southern end of **Los Cristianos (Wp.1, 0M)**, we follow the tarmac lane down to a walled villa to swing left and follow the beach path along to an *Espacio Naturaleza Protegido* sign **(Wp.2)**, where we climb up onto a path to start zigzagging up the cliffs. Alternatively, walk along in front of new villas to new stone steps and climb up a path to the traditional route. Our well-marked path gets rougher as we climb, passing a new path coming in from the left **(Wp.3)** and the surface changes from dirt to broken rock, until the route turns into a cleft **(Wp.4, 13M)** approximately half way up the cliffs; if you look towards **Los Cristianos** at this point, you will be facing directly towards the **Princesa Dacil Hotel**.

We take a faint path which climbs away from the main walking route **(SW)** to pass a small cave **(Wp.5, 16M)** as we climb above our earlier route, and our path becomes more defined. Up through a hairpin bend, we continue up into the plateau to go over a crest and meander into a shallow valley to a T-junction with another path (**Wp.6, 23M**). We go right (**SW**) to follow the path over to the *parapente* launch point on a bald knoll (**Wp.7**) marked by tattered wind flags. We go **SW** on a path which drops into a *barranco*, and then climb its southern side back up onto the plateau to curve around the cliffs before turning into a valley (**Wp.8, 30M**), where our path contours round to cross the watercourse and bring us back above the sea. Our path wanders through a landscape of tumbled valleys (**SSW**) which drop into the sea on our right until we meet a larger *barranco*. Small shale heaps show that this was a stone cutting area, as we head inland past a shattered rock before crossing the *barranco* floor (**Wp.9, 35M**) and heading seawards. Before reaching the sea, our route swings left (**S**) into a small valley littered with shale

Looking north from the Guaza plateau.

heaps. Cresting a small rise, we see a large stone quarry on the far side of a valley. We curve left to descend into the valley and cross the stream bed (**Wp.10, 40M**) below a second quarry.

Although the main path leads off to the further quarry, we look for a path on our left (**Wp.11**) which climbs up alongside this quarry to become clearer when we are upon the plateau. Now it is easy strolling (**SSE**) past a path off to the left (**Wp.12, 44M**) by the remains of a cairn, for us to come to the top of the cliffs (**Wp.13**) overlooking **La Arenita** beach. In a few metres we meet a path coming from the plateau on our left (**Wp.14**), and a small quarry is on our right at the top of the cliffs. On the path, we go right and left past a substantial cairn, to start descending the wall of a valley. This is an adventurous descent, and care is needed due to the loose stones which litter the generally well-made path. We wind down the wall of this sharp valley towards the beach, our route taking to bare rock where a section of path has fallen away (**Wp.15**). The path drops steeply down below a burnt orange rock outcrop for an almost scrambling descent before our route runs out into a tumbled landscape to a '*pa*' sign (**Wp.16**). We swing down an old dirt road to arrive on a dirt road which runs alongside the large pebble beach. Turning left, we are just an easy stroll away from the seaward face of **Palm Mar (60M)**. If you want to take a break at this point, head inland onto the 'main' road, and behind the **Trattoria** restaurant you will find **Bar Super**, a modern version of a rustic *tipico* for snacks and drinks.

PALM MAR TO FARO DE RASCA

On the seaward side of **Palm Mar (0M)** we head **SSW** along a dirt road to come onto a new road by the **Playa La Arenita** beach sign (**Wp.17, 10M**). In

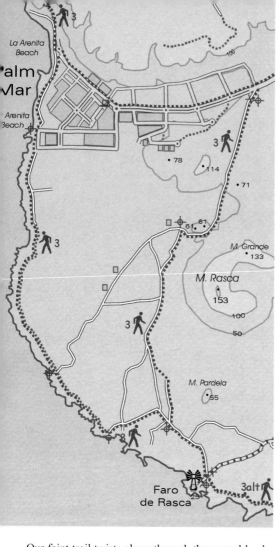

a few metres the broad new road swings left so we go right onto a coastal track (**Wp.18**) to go over a jagged volcanic point and undulate along the lava coastline (**S**) passing narrow dirt roads off to our left (**Wp.19, 15M**) and (**Wp.20, 17M**), until the dirt road finishes (**Wp.21**), for us to continue on a narrow path which comes onto a small flood plain with a boulder wall on its seaward side (**Wp.22**). Towards the end of the wall, we step through a tumbled section onto a dirt road that runs down to the sea. Looking left (**S**) we spot the narrow coastal walking trail threading its way through the volcanic boulders, with the sea breaking on the lava shoreline on our right.

Our faint trail twists along through the surreal landscape with a substantial boulder wall 50m inland of us as we cross a dirt road and come to a '*pa*' sign above a pocket in the shoreline (**Wp.23, 30M**). A boulder with a red bull's-eye marks our path's continuation through the *malpais* past rock shelters and a pair of foaming inlets. Across a sandy area, we continue amongst tumbled lava and over a ridge crowned with rock shelters which overlooks a pretty bay. Our route is **SSW** to crest another ridge and come to a junction overlooking another picturesque bay (**44M**).

Now we head inland on a rough rock road (**Wp.24**) onto a flood plain (**Wp.25**). We follow the dirt road heading inland to a junction of dirt roads (**Wp.26**). Keeping straight on, we cross another junction (**Wp.27**) and pass another dirt road off to our left (**Wp.28**) before our route climbs up to join the *faro*'s tarmac access road (**Wp.29**) for us to stroll the few metres to the **Faro de Rasca (Wp.30, 55M)**. The lighthouse area is a pleasant spot to take a break overlooking the *malpais* and volcanic bays pounded by the Atlantic Ocean.

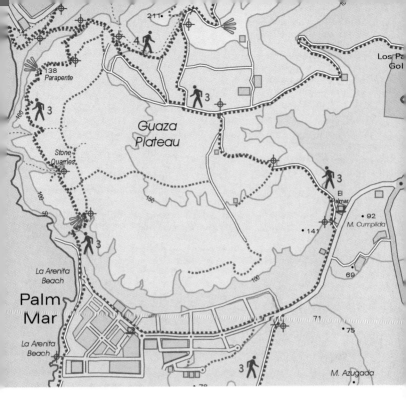

FARO DE RASCA TO LOS CRISTIANOS

Refreshed (**0M**), we retrace our route down into the *malpais* until we come to the second dirt road junction (**Wp.27**) where we go right (**N**). At the end of the dirt road where it turns back on itself (**Wp.31**), we cut across the open *malpais* (**NW**) to strike a dirt road (**Wp.32**) for us to head **N**. Past dirt roads off to our left (**Wps.33 & 34**), our dirt road curves around **Montaña Rasca** with a low stone wall on our right. It is easy strolling across the plain, passing more dirt roads off to our left (**Wps.35 & 36**) before we come up to a T-junction (**Wp.37**).

Going right, we start climbing on the rough road to pass a '*pa*' sign (**Wp.38, 25M**) and continue ascending between red hills before curving left to cross a gentle plain ringed by small hills. Our road climbs gently up through a pass in the red hills to drop into a second plain with a fruit plantation away on our right. A second gentle climb through a second pass brings us up to overlook the **Palm Mar** road and a gentle stroll down past the locked vehicle barrier (**Wp.39, 37M**).

We walk inland on the tarmac passing a walled bungalow, to just before **El Palmar** where we find an old dirt road marked by a '*pa*' sign (**Wp.40, 47M**) which climbs up onto the **Guaza Plateau**. The chain barrier by the '*pa*' sign is superfluous as the road has eroded to the stage of being impassable to vehicles. It is a hard slog up what remains of the road to climb above the restaurant and banana plantations as we curve towards the west

A large cairn (**Wp.41**) marks the end of the main climb as the gradient moderates to bring us up onto the plateau (**Wp.42, 63M**). Here, by a small cairn, we step through a tumbled wall onto a walking trail lined with stones, to come onto a dirt road (**Wp.43**). Our dirt road curves towards **Mount Guaza** (**N**) bringing us up to a T-junction below the farm (**Wp.44**) where we go left (**W**). When the main dirt road goes right (**Wp.45**) we continue straight ahead on a dirt road which curves round abandoned terraces. After descending gently, the dirt road swings left (**Wp.46, 82M**) as we continue ahead on a walking trail to come onto the main path up from **Los Cristianos**. Once on the main path, it is all downhill - not that this is a relaxing section as the loose rocks littering the route demand care for every step. Halfway down the cliff face, we meet our outward route to retrace our step back to the **Costamar Apartments**, 105 minutes (**105M**) from **Faro de Rasca**.

ALTERNATIVE FINISH - FARO DE RASCA TO LAS GALLETAS

This route forms a section of our coastal route which links to **Las Galletas** and the start of our **Los Abrigos** route. This section starts well but becomes uninspiring, so look forward to the sea front restaurants.

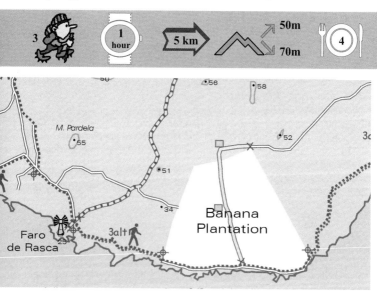

To the east (**E**) of the *faro* is a huge covered banana plantation, and our first target is the seaward corner of this great tented structure. From **Faro de Rasca** we walk to the vehicle barrier on the tarmac lane and swing right (**Wp.1**) down a rough sloping track.

From the bottom of the slope, a faint walking trail meanders eastwards (**E**) through the rocks before climbing up to a '*pa*' sign post, at which point we drop down onto a broad dirt road on the seaward corner of the plantation

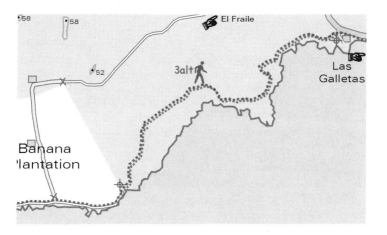

(**Wp.2**). We stroll (**E**) between the massive foundations of the plantations and an impressive rocky coastline for over a kilometre, passing a tarmac plantation road (**Wp.3**) before coming to the end of the dirt road and plantation (**Wp.4**). We squeeze around a palm tree to enter an area of *malpais* where agriculture was abandoned decades ago.

We head north-east (**NE**) to pass the crumbling walls of old plantations on our left (**Wp.5**) and then on our right, before swinging east-north-east (**ENE**) to pass an old water channel on our left (**Wp.6**). The *malpais* is featureless although confused by a myriad of dirt tracks. Keeping the town of **El Fraile** on our left, we head approximately east (**E**) to **Wp.9**, although our own route passes through **Wp.7** and then through **Wp.8** to look across to the red doors of the **Cruz Roja** (Red Cross) building. Walking trails take us past little bays and unofficial camping areas to reach the **Cruz Roja** car park (**Wp10**). We now have an easy stroll along the pavement to **Las Galletas** for refreshments in one of the sea front restaurants.

LINK FROM LAS GALLETAS TO THE START OF THE LOS ABRIGOS ROUTE

Walk east (**E**) through **Las Galletas** to come onto the main road heading north (**Wp.11**). Head inland, then turn off at the **Ten Bel Commercial Centre** (**Wp.12**), to walk east (**E**) and then north (**N**) to the **Chapparal Commercial Centre** with its totem poles (**Wp.13**). Continue east (**E**), passing **Chayofita** on your left and coming to the traffic island (**Wp.14**). From this point, choose either to go left then right, or right then left, to reach the alternative start points of the route to **Los Abrigos**, Walk 5, 'Coastal Escapism'.

4. MOUNT GUAZA

Seen from the motorway, **Mount Guaza** appears inaccessible and so it is - but our route takes us up from the **Guaza Plateau** on an easy, but very strenuous, climb to the summit (428 metres). Being so close to **Los Cristianos**, and 'because it is there', many people climb to the summit by accident; unbelievable once you have done it, but true.

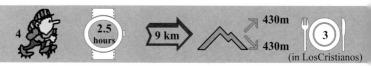

4 | 2.5 hours | 9 km | 430m / 430m | 3 (in LosCristianos)

We start at the new walking trail between the **Playa Graciosa** and **Paradise Park** developments on the edge of **Los Cristianos** (**Wp.1, 0M**) by taking the steps down into the water runoff and set off on the nicely manicured path for a gentle stroll up to join the traditional walking trail (**Wp.2, 3M**).

Turning uphill, we start climbing seriously up through a zigzag, the path getting rougher while **Los Cristianos** gets smaller, for us to pass the turn off of our **Palm Mar** route (**Wp.3, 8M**). The going gets rougher as we come to a tempting path straight ahead (**Wp.4, 13M**) where we climb right on the main path. We keep climbing with our route swinging right to follow the *barranco* and pass paths off to our right (**Wps.5 & 6**) before coming to the junction (**Wp.7, 16M**) with our return from **Faro de Rasca** route.

Here we continue straight on, thankfully gradient free, beside an old water channel along the lip of the *barranco* until our path starts climbing up through the tumbled walls of old terraces (**Wp.8**) before returning to the *barranco*'s lip. More climbing up through old terraces, including a section where the path splits in two (**Wp.9**) before rejoining, brings us up to the end of an old dirt road (**Wp.10, 21M**). We swing left to walk up a path facing the intimidating bulk of the mountain, with the *barranco* dropping away on our left, to slog our way up to join the **Mount Guaza** dirt road (**Wp.11, 27M**).

If you thought it was energetic so far - well, now it gets tougher as we slog up the wide and dusty dirt road, passing an old walking trail on our left before passing the vehicle barrier (**Wp.12**). The road swings right after the barrier for us to climb up to a hairpin bend with panoramic views, **Los Palos Golf** standing out like an emerald jewel amongst the dull, tented banana plantations.

After a break for the views it is back to slogging uphill with hills on our right, a *barranco* on our left and a seemingly endless ascent ahead on the dusty road. Cresting a rise (**Wp.13, 39M**) we have a short section of downhill before the ascent is rejoined. Finally the tops of aerials come into view as we walk up to a junction (**Wp.14, 56M**) where a new dirt road sweeps left around the *caldera*. Straight ahead, we climb up the old road to pass a large cairn (**Wp.15**) and then a final steep slog brings us up to the Trig point amongst the old transmitters (**Wp.16, 63M**).

Technically this is the top of our route, but not the end as after a break to

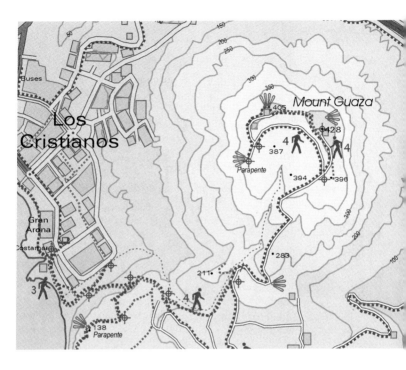

recover we continue down the old jeep trail (**0M**) to come down to the second set of transmitters (**Wp.17**) for views over **Playa de Las Américas**. Now it is easy strolling along the new dirt road past the newest transmitters and down to a junction (**Wp.18**) where we go out to a *parapente* launch point for views over **Los Cristianos (Wp.19)** and our start point way below us.

Back on the dirt road an easy stroll and gentle uphill bring us back to the junction with our outward route (**Wp.14, 20M**). Now it is all downhill (!) remembering to take as much care on the descent as the ascent, particularly on the very rough path down from the plateau, and we are back at our start point after **145 minutes,** including a 17 minute break (to recover) at the Trig point.

5. COASTAL ESCAPISM

This coastal walk is deceptively interesting, with its dramatic coastline quite in contrast to the boring landscape inland from our route. A good hike to work up an appetite for lunch in the **Los Abrigos** seafood restaurants, or as an escape from the golf developments; take your choice, but it is tougher than it looks. You can finish the walk at **Los Abrigos**, in which case time and distance are approximately halved.

Full Route
(halve time, distance, ascents & descents if finishing in **Los Abrigos**)

3 | 3.25 hours | 14 km | 100m / 100m | 4

Choose your starting point

Our start point in **Costa del Silencio** depends on the sea conditions. If the sea is turbulent we start at **Coral Mar** (**Wpt.1A**) and walk across to the *Espacio Naturaleza Protegido* sign to follow a clear path alongside a wall around the base of **Montaña Amarilla** which undulates gently along, passing a path off right (**Wpt.2A**). We continue until we come just above a barrier to our left on a dirt road (**Wpt.3A**), where we head downhill and seawards, passing a junction of dirt roads (**Wpt.4A**) while looking for another *Espacio Naturaleza Protegido* sign down on our left (**Wpt.5A**). This marks the 'official' path which we reach in the maze of dirt roads and paths in this confused area (**Wpt.8, 12M**).

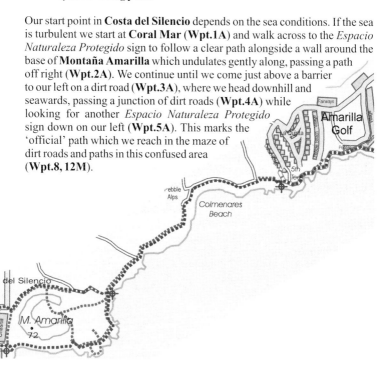

When the sea is quiet and at low tide, we start off from the pebble beach below **Chasna** to follow the shoreline around the rocks below **Montaña Amarilla**. We pass an *Espacio Naturaleza Protegido* sign and **Montaña Amarilla** on the left (**Wpt.1, 4M**), and begin to negotiate the rocks (popular with naturists at weekends and holidays, so watch where you put those boots), taking care as they are slippery.

The slippery rocks end (**Wpt.2, 9M**) and we climb a slope of rock to ascend onto the headland, where we find the coastal path (**Wpt.3, 16M**) which winds around between the impressive coastline and the *malpais* inland, before dropping down to the "pa" sign in a gully.

Once on the official path, route finding is easy. We pass a junction of paths (**Wpt.4**) where a staired route climbs **Montaña Amarilla** and another route goes left as we continue along the coast. A path runs off right to run around the headland (**Wpt.5, 18M**) as our walking trail meanders through this *malpais* landscape with the rugged coastline on our right, passing another cross roads of paths (**Wpt.6, 20M**). Now **Amarilla Golf, Golf del Sur** and **Los Abrigos** come into view ahead. A path runs back left towards **Montaña Amarilla** (**Wpt.7, 24M**) as we join our alternative starting point (**Wpt.8**) near a '*pa*' sign.

Yet another start is to climb **Montaña Amarilla** (steeper than it looks, and dangerous if windy) to the summit and then follow the right hand path around the rim of the *caldera* before dropping down and heading seawards to pick up the coastal path.

The onward route

A dirt track comes in from the left (**Wpt.9, 29M**), and then vegetation begins, with *tabaiba* and prickly pear each side of the path (**Wpt.10, 31M**). Our path turns inland into a pebble dunes area (**Wpt.11, 35M**) with a pebble 'alps' inland, as we come down towards the bay of **Playa Colmenares**.

Wild, unspoilt views on 'Coastal Escapism'.

It is a wobbly walk across the pebbles to come onto a dirt road which drops us down behind the beach with a dirt road coming in from the left (**Wpt.12, 44M**). Following the road, or wobbly walking along the pebble beach, brings us to the end of the bay where we head between the sea and a lagoon to pick up the **Amarilla Golf** coastal path (**Wpt.13, 47M**).

This well made path has the steepest ascents and descents of the whole route as it runs along the impressive coastline at the edge of the golf development. We pass a dirt road (**Wpt. 14**) which runs left into **Amarilla Golf** as we continue on the coastal path, passing the 5th tee (**Wpt.15**) on the left. The path takes us past apartments and a road off on our left (**Wpt.16, 52M**) and then a path left (**Wpt.17**), which short cuts the ridge after waypoint 16 before running out at the entrance to the marina (**Wpt.18, 64M**).

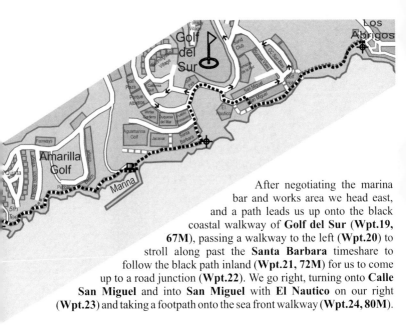

After negotiating the marina bar and works area we head east, and a path leads us up onto the black coastal walkway of **Golf del Sur** (**Wpt.19, 67M**), passing a walkway to the left (**Wpt.20**) to stroll along past the **Santa Barbara** timeshare to follow the black path inland (**Wpt.21, 72M**) for us to come up to a road junction (**Wpt.22**). We go right, turning onto **Calle San Miguel** and into **San Miguel** with **El Nautico** on our right (**Wpt.23**) and taking a footpath onto the sea front walkway (**Wpt.24, 80M**).

A pleasant stroll along this impressive sea front brings us to the **Golf Hotel** (**Wpt.25, 85M**) and a road off left to **San Blas Centro Comercial**. Our path runs around the seaward side of the hotel, the end of **Golf del Sur**, for a staired descent to **Playa San Blas** (**Wpt.26**). We stroll down behind the pebbles before the path climbs out of the valley with a lagoon on our right (**Wpt.27, 90M**) and **Los Abrigos** ahead.

Across the headland, we have a semi-staired descent to the beach before ascending on a paved walkway to the edge of **Los Abrigos** (**Wpt.28, 97M**) where we have a choice of bars and restaurants for refreshments. If you would prefer to ride back, regular bus services run between **Los Abrigos** and the resorts of **Costa del Silencio**, **Los Cristianos** and **Playa de las Américas**.

Our return to **Los Cristianos** follows the same route, but as we approach **Montaña Amarilla** we have the alternative of following the base of the mountain on its inland (**N**) side. To take this alternative route, at the end of the dirt road leaving the *protegido* area marked by the signpost (**Wpt.5A**) we begin to turn inland, passing a junction of dirt roads (**Wpt.4A**).

Just before a gate across the dirt road we take an easy path which runs around the base of the mountain (**Wpt.3A**), ignoring a path off left (**Wpt.2A**) which runs into the *caldera*. As we enter the buildings of **Costa del Silencio**, we leave the path round the mountain near the **Chasna** building (**Wpt.1A**) to walk the few metres south (**S**) back to our start point (**3H 15M**).

6. PICOS LAS AMÉRICAS

In **Playa de las Américas**, the mountains are on your doorstep - actually, your back doorstep, as our energetic but most rewarding route reveals. This route also links with the **TS-11**, giving options to continue on to **Adeje** (Walk 8) or **Arona** (Walk 7), 'DownTo Town'.

The geology is interesting, but the demands of the final section make it suitable for experienced mountain walkers only.

Town Section

Starting from the busy **San Eugenio** roundabout, we walk up the street heading inland past the **Las Dalias Hotel (Wp.1)**, to cross the motorway to a T-junction (**Wp.2, 5M**). Going right in 50 metres, we turn onto a broad tiled path (**Wp.3**) to climb steeply up between the **Vista Mar** and **Roque Villas** developments, to arrive breathless back on **Avenida Europa (Wp.4)**. A steady uphill stroll takes us onto **Calle Suecia (Wp.5)** and up to another wide, steep, staired ascent (**Wp.6**), for us to emerge at the **Calle Portugal** junction (**Wp.7, 15M**). Now it is onwards and upwards as we slog up **Avenida Europa** to turn right (**Wp.8**) just before **Ocean View** for the last slog up to the ridge road (**Wp.9, 20M**).

After the steep ascent, we are rewarded by an easy stroll towards the **Picos (W)** which are dramatically silhouetted against the bulk of **Roque del Conde** (Walk 14). There are sweeping views down over **Playa de las Américas** on our left, and the banana-filled *caldera* on our right, passing roads off to the left (**Wps. 10&11**) as we come up to the parking area (**Wp.12, 25M**). Car users could cut out the energetic climbs by driving up to this point, so for the mountains section of the route we take the times from the car parking area.

Picos Section

Due to the exposed nature of the route, it should not be attempted in windy weather.

From the end of the tarmac (**Wp.1, 0M**), a track leads around a water tank before narrowing to a walking trail which climbs steeply up to **The Pimple** (**259 metres, Wp.2, 8M**). Take particular care in ascending and descending **The Pimple**. The grit-covered nature of the route can result in the rock becoming slippery, and can easily upset the unwary. After taking in the panoramic views, we stroll down to the saddle to begin ascending the first peak. Soon after the start of the climb, we need to swing left at a junction marked by a cairn (**Wp.3**) to continue steeply upwards.

The path up to the first peak is not always clear, but if in doubt, climb up towards the highest point that you can see. The steep ascent eases as we come alongside the peak (**Wp.4, 14M**), from which point a short scramble takes us up to the 350 metre high rock platform.

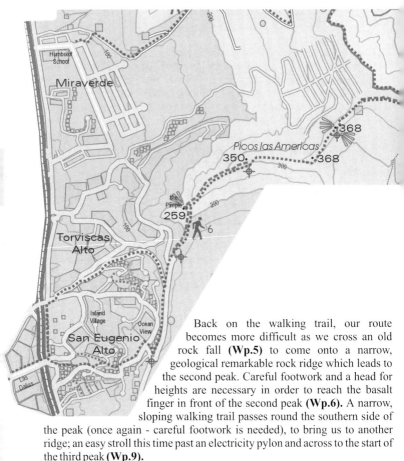

Back on the walking trail, our route becomes more difficult as we cross an old rock fall **(Wp.5)** to come onto a narrow, geological remarkable rock ridge which leads to the second peak. Careful footwork and a head for heights are necessary in order to reach the basalt finger in front of the second peak **(Wp.6)**. A narrow, sloping walking trail passes round the southern side of the peak (once again - careful footwork is needed), to bring us to another ridge; an easy stroll this time past an electricity pylon and across to the start of the third peak **(Wp.9)**.

Our trail leads up in a steady climb to the small plateau at 368 metres altitude **(Wp.10, 35M)** - now that is what we call a panoramic view! We return by retracing our outward route to the tarmac road, and then the choice of descents into the resort.

Link to the TS-11 route to Adeje or Arona

Once on the third peak, we are close to the TS-11 **Arona-Adeje** walking route. To link to the TS-11, continue along the ridge north-east (**NE**) to its end, again taking care with footwork. We then descend on its western side in an easy scramble to relatively flat ground **(Wp.11)**. A faint trail with the remains of a stone wall on our right, pushes through the undergrowth to bring us to an abandoned cottage **(Wp.13)**. Beyond the cottage, a broad trail brings us onto the dirt *pista* of the TS-11 **(Wp.14)**.

7. DOWN TO TOWN

The TS-11 is one of the old donkey trail routes which links **Arona** and **Adeje** although the old route has unfortunately been disrupted by high level developments in **Torviscas Alto**. For the eastern arm, we have an easy country walk with impressive views, followed by the **Picos Las Américas** route for our descent into the resort, or in wet or windy weather walk down through the new developments to finish in **Torviscas**. Start with a relaxed ascent to **Arona** on the 480 Titsa bus service.

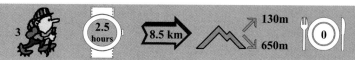

3   2.5 hours   8.5 km   130m / 650m   0

We start from the **Arona** bus terminus (**Wp.1, 0M**) by strolling up the **Calle Duque de la Torre** paved street to the town square (**Wp.2**) and go left across the square to walk up the top road to cross the TF-51 onto the **Vento** road (**Wp.3, 8M**). Walking up the **Vento** road, we pass **Casa del Pintur** on our right before our route runs down to the Obelisk junction (**Wp.4**) in **Vento**. Going left we pass the **Roque del Conde** path (**Wp.5, 18M**) just before going left on a *camino rural* tarmaced road.

The narrow road drops down through abandoned terraces, passing an impressive house (**Wp.6**), before coming down to a junction where another *camino rural* goes right across the *barranco* (**Wp.7**). After a short uphill houses line the road and we drop steeply down to the TF-51 main road (**Wp.8**). Watching out for traffic, we turn right to walk down the road past the 3km marker to an old loop of the road (**Wp.9**) and on to the start of **Camino Viejo de Adeje (Wp.10, 38M**) dirt road.

On the dirt road, we sweep down to cross the watercourse of the first *barranco* (**Wp.11**). We climb up to pass an abandoned house on our left (**Wp.12**) before the cobbled trail zigzags down to cross the **Barranco del Rey** (**Wp.13**) . A steady climb brings us up to meet the friendly dogs of a

Beside the water channel on the TS-11, prickly pear (left), *kleinia nerifolia* and *euphorbia canariensis* (right).

neat-walled farm (**Wp.14, 53M**). Passing the farm on our left, we stroll across the gentle slopes towards a low ridge which ends in a rocky outcrop. Passing a T-junction (**Wp.15**) where a dirt road goes right towards a white cottage, we continue ahead on the water-eroded trail which improves as we stroll up to meet a water channel on the ridge (**Wp.16, 60M**) from where we have spectacular views down over a *caldera* to **Los Cristianos** and **Playa de las Américas**.

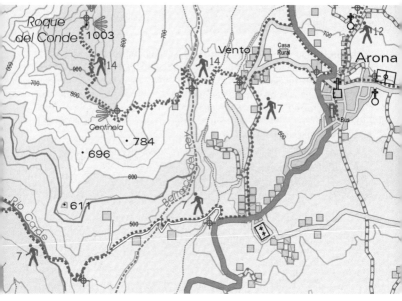

This ridge may seem fairly insignificant when seen from the east, but we face a steep descent on its west side. We zigzag down a donkey trail, its loose stone surface making for a slow, skittery descent until we cross a large working water canal (**Wp.17, 69M**) known locally as the **Rio Conde**. Now we are on a gentle dirt path which runs alongside the **Rio Conde** to give us an easy stroll along to a dirt road junction (**Wp.18**), where we turn downhill to a second junction (**Wp.19**). The main dirt road runs down to the water treatment works on the floor of the *caldera*, while we go right on a fainter trail onto a saddle (**Wp.20**) between a water change point on the canal, and the **Picos las Américas** on our left (**85M**).

Infrastructure and development have cut the traditional TS11 route, and we have three alternatives:
A

Picos Las Américas Route
Go left (**S**) past the abandoned cottage to climb up onto the third peak of **Picos las Américas**, and follow this route across the exposed ridges (do not attempt in windy or wet weather) to the road system above **San Eugenio Alto** (**30-40M**), from where you have a choice of routes into the resort areas.

B
Go down into the development, and follow the roads down to the entrance of **Balcones del Conde** (**15-20M**). Note that the road entrance may be closed at weekends below the current development works (November 2002).

C
Go up to the **Rio Conde**, easiest from the first dirt road junction (**Wp.18**) and follow the canal above the development to meet our '**Adeje Skywalker**' route. We then have options to descend to the **Fañabe** area or to continue on the **Adeje Skywalker** route to **Adeje**.

8. ADEJE SKYWALKER

This is a spectacular new route with awesome views at almost every turn, but it comes at a price. While most of the route involves easy walking on a paved water canal, the **Rio Conde**, we have to cross an extremely vertiginous aqueduct and edge around a mountain above sheer drops; a good head for heights and sure-footedness are essential. We named this route, 'Adeje Skywalker' for its elevated views over the south of Tenerife with the impression of being suspended above these southern landscapes.

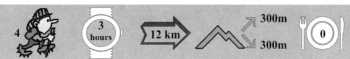

We start out from the bus stop by the **Adeje** *cementario* (cemetery), and in a few steps we go right onto a dirt road **(Wp.1),** passing an archaeological sign. Our dirt road winds down into the *barranco* to cross the water course **(Wp.2)** and come to a dirt cross roads.

We go over at the cross-roads to walk up the higher dirt road, passing through a metal gate **(Wp.3)** as we climb up onto the ridge at a U-bend **(Wp.4, 12M)**. Now the dirt road heads up the line of the ridge, passing a white cottage on our right and coming up to a junction just past a water tank **(Wp.5, 333m alt, 20M)**. Water pipes cross our route as we continue straight ahead on the dirt road towards the mountains. The road becomes rougher as we climb the mountains, passing *Naturaleza* signs **(Wp.6, 364m alt)** until we come to a faint path marked by a cairn **(Wp.7, 398m alt, 30M)** where the rough dirt road swings west **(W)**.

Taking the narrow path, we continue our steady ascent **(NE)** through the shrub-covered slopes, passing a small cairn **(Wp.8),** our path becoming

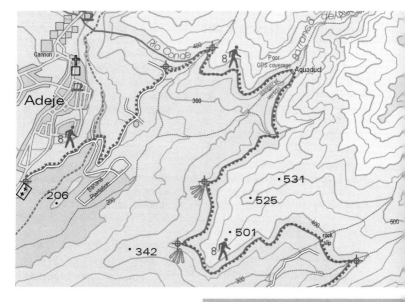

fainter as we gradually close with the canal. Finally we clamber up onto the canal (**Wp.9, 422m alt**) for a relaxing break after the long ascent of slogging up dirt roads and narrow paths.

We are on a broad (approximately 1m wide) paved water canal which gives us an elevated walkway with sensational views - surprisingly, unknown to other walking writers. This is an easy walking surface, but take care to 'look where you walk, and STOP to look at the views', as there is no protection from the drops alongside the canal. An easy stroll takes us over a small bridge **(Wp.10)** before curving round into a smaller *barranco* to cross its water course on another bridge (**Wp.11, 50M**), and walking out to a viewpoint **(Wp.12).**

As the canal turns into the next *barranco* it becomes vertiginous, with sheer drops on our right and a cliff on our left causing poor GPS coverage. If you have any doubts over this section, return towards **Adeje**.

We walk up to the major obstacle on our route, an aqueduct **(Wp.13)** carrying the canal over the steep **Barranco del Agua**, which drops down from **Roque Abinque.** In this dramatic orogenic setting of soaring mountains, cliffs and sheer *barrancos*, we edge over the thirty metre span, to a well-deserved rest at its eastern end (**60M**). After recovering from the aqueduct crossing, we soon face another vertiginous section where the canal runs under a cliff and there are some missing slabs; here we step onto the black water pipe to carefully negotiate these sections.

Turning out of the main **Barranco del Agua** ravine, we cross a small bridge **(Wp.14)** to enter a landscape of gentler slopes. After another bridge **(Wp.15)** we walk out to a *mirador* view (**Wp.16, 78M**) as the **Rio Conde** swings left. A steel water pipe crosses the canal **(Wp.17),** just before we cross the **Morro Grueso** ridge **(Wp.18)** to swing above the **Fañabe** valley. We curve left **(Wp.19)** to see the **Rio Conde** sweeping around the broad valley ahead of us.

Easy strolling takes us past a small cave (**Wp.20, 95M**) and over a small bridge **(Wp.21),** before we come to a section where rocks and earth cover the canal **(Wp.22).** Picking our way over the rock, we come back onto the paved canal to pass a dirt road on our right **(Wp.23)** and cross a small bridge **(Wp.24)** before coming to a water change point (**Wp.25, 110M**) where we drop down onto a dirt road which runs alongside the canal. We follow the dirt road until it swings right to drop into the valley **(Wp.26)** where we clamber back onto the paved canal. After crossing a bridge and a small canal which crosses the **Rio Conde**, we come to a difficult water change point **(Wp.27).**

Some nimble footwork is needed to negotiate the inland scrub and change point to get back onto the paved canal. As we stroll on, the dirt road alongside the canal turns away towards an abandoned cottage on the saddle between two valleys **(Wp.28),** and we then climb over a small rock slip **(Wp.29)** and take care where there are occasional missing slabs, before we are below the 'White House' which sits above water change points which are numbered 195-9 and 194-8 (**Wp.30, 124M**). A couple of minutes later, the canal passes underground and is crossed by means of the rough dirt access road to the 'White House' **(Wp.31)** which gives us the choice of an uphill diversion to one of the region's most noticeable but least visited landmarks.

On the Rio Conde, high above the southern coast.

Now we leave the **Rio Conde** to head down the rough dirt road past a large water tank (**Wp.32**) on our left, to a junction of dirt roads (**Wp.33, 140M**), signed TS11 on our right. The dirt road is littered with shale and scree, making for slow skittery progress down past water tanks, those to the left (**Wp.34**) old and empty, and new and fenced to the right (**Wp.35**), before the dirt road heads straight down the side of the valley. Our walking surface improves as we pass dirt roads, to the left (**Wp.36**) and on the right (**Wp.37**), before we reach the first house and a tarmac lane (**Wp.38, 165M**). As we stroll down, we pass the impressive entrance to **Finca Amapola de Fañabe** (**Wp.39**) and then come onto the new road system behind the **Humbolt School** (**Wp.40, 170M**).

From here we can head past the school (**W**) on our left, to reach the access road alongside the motorway, or alternatively turn south (**S**) to follow the new roads towards the centre of the resort. (See the street plans in 'A Drive! Tenerife Touring Map for possible finish routes into the resort area.)

Alternative Finishes

Alternative finishes involve continuing on the **Rio Conde** to the new developments and then heading down to **Torviscas Alto** on the new road system, or continuing past the new developments to join up with the eastern arm of the TS-11 to follow the **Picos Las Américas** route down into the resort.

9. TAUCHO TOUR

A circular walk with a surprise finish - sounds improbable, but for Taucho Tour it's true. This is an easy route on old donkey trails taking in spectacular views, excellent flora including an unusual floral phenomenon, and after a rather unpromising start the landscape exudes a bucolic charm; in short idyllic walking country, and with a classic *tipico* (**Bar Taucho**) not far away.

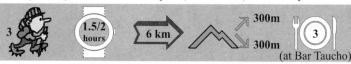

3 | 1.5/2 hours | 6 km | 300m / 300m | 3 (at Bar Taucho)

We start by driving west on the TF1 motorway and continue past the **Adeje** roundabout onto the TF82 and look for a right turning (easily missed) onto the TF583 road to **Taucho**. After the twisting, 3rd gear, ascent follow the narrow road through the village past the bus terminus (and **Bar Taucho**) and continue on the *camino rural* until you come to the church on your left and a parking area. Despite the bus terminus, TITSA's timetable does not include any services to the village!

From the corner of the church square (**Wp.1, 0M**) we stroll along **Calle La Serrería** before leaving it to go right (**Wp.2**) onto a smaller *camino rural*. Down into a small valley, the tarmac goes left to houses as we step right onto a broad dirt road (**Wp.3**) to continue (**S**) past large steel gates (**Wp.4**). Just after the gates a dirt *pista* goes left while we stay on the main dirt road which runs along to swing into a floriferous valley with a walking trail crossing the valley below us. We cross the valley's water course (**Wp.5**) to come gently uphill and meet the walking trail just before some steel gates.

Going left (**Wp.6**), we clamber up over rock to come onto the donkey trail's continuation as it skirts a fenced area, passing gates and an *embalse* (**Wp.7**), to come onto another dirt road. Soon we take a walking trail off to the right (**Wp.8**) alongside a small *barranco*, which soon curves right to cross the *barranco* floor (**Wp.9**) and then we come onto a dirt road arriving from the left (**Wp.10**). We swing along to a *parapente* launch point (**Wp.11**), with a most unusual official sign, to continue on a walking trail dropping into a steeper *barranco*. Across the watercourse (**Wp.12**), we climb up the southern wall, crossing a side *barranco* (**Wp.13**) for a final ascent to **Lomo de las Lajas** (**Wp.14, 28M**) with its impressive views over **Adeje** and the coast.

Leaving **Lomo de las Lajas**, we go east (**E**) to pick up the eroded walking trail (our 'Queen Of The South' route, and if you want really spectacular views go right to the top of the small ridge but take care) which climbs steadily and curves left for us to come up to a gentle open ridge (**Wp.15**) ahead of us.

A path takes us up the left side of the ridge ('Queen Of The South' route is a few metres to our right) in a steady climb, crossing a rock section (**Wp.16**) before coming onto the 'Queen Of The South' route. Continuing the steady climb, we come amongst the pines on a well defined path to reach a junction (**Wp.17, 47M**). Going left, we pass a large green dot to climb up to an **Ifonche** route sign on the crest of the ridge (**Wp.18**) with its carved water channels.

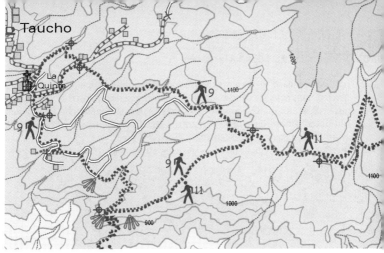

Green dots guide us west (**W**) on a faint path which zigzags down to the floor of the small valley (**Wp.19**), with an old cottage above us on our right, and then gently climbs up to cross a small ridge where we meet a steel water pipe (**Wp.20**). Now our path follows the water pipe steeply down into this unusual *barranco*. The *barranco* floor is completely choked with brambles which stretch as far as we can see in a great green phalanx we have not seen anywhere else. We zigzag down before following the southern side to cross the watercourse (**Wp.21, 58M**), at a cutting through the brambles, before climbing up over an old water canal to ascend the northern side still accompanied by the water pipe. As we climb to move away from the valley the bramble-choked watercourse is even more impressive until we turn away (**Wp.22**) to drop into another valley to cross its watercourse just below a mature pine (**Wp.23**), before a steady climb up for our path to cross open ground (**Wp.24**).

Houses are ahead of us as we descend alongside the pipe into another small valley (**Wp.25**) and climb up the path to cross open ground and into a minor valley (**Wp.26**) before climbing up the rough stone trail between stone walls to reach a *camino rural* (**Wp.27**) opposite a pair of houses. From here you can shortcut down the *camino rural* to the church, but we will go for a surprise finish.

Across the *camino rural* the water pipe continues past the fence of house Nº21, with its noisy dog. At first this looks an unlikely route but as we drop down the donkey trail emerges for us to descend steeply down its boulder-laid surface into the **Barranco de la Quinta**. Zigzags bring us steeply down, taking care on the slippery pine needles by a mature pine (**Wp.28**), to come onto the valley floor (**Wp.29**) at the bottom of the sheer-sided *barranco*. Green dots indicate a narrow path down the *barranco* floor, the rough boulders giving way to an easier surface before we emerge onto tarmac between **Taucho** and **La Quinta** (**Wp.30**). Ignoring a green arrow, we go left on the tarmac for a few metres to the start of a stone-laid trail (**Wp.31**) with a wooden handrail. The trail starts steeply and gets steeper as it zigzags up the *barranco* wall; far too steep for a safe descent. Puffing and panting, we come up to the back of a white cottage for the final climb up onto a dirt road where our start point is a few metres away on our right (**93M**) - now isn't that better than an easy finish!

10. WOW! SPECTACULAR

Just occasionally a walking route comes to light which has everything; spectacular views, awesome scenery, magnificent flora. Wow! Spectacular is just such a route, and has been missed by all other walking writers. If you only had time for one Tenerife walk, and are sure-footed with a head for heights, this is the route you should choose.

Do not attempt this route in wet or windy weather.

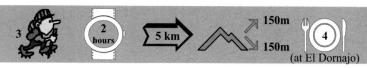

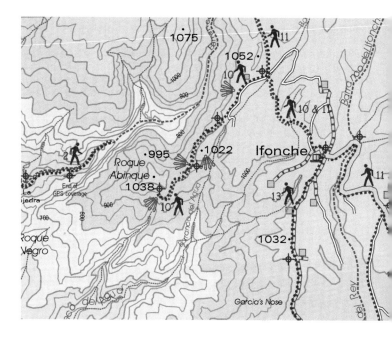

We start alongside **El Dornajo** in **Ifonche** (**Wp.1, 0M**), to stroll down the tarmac lane (**W**) and turn right (**Wp.2**) onto a dirt road and then onto a *sendero* at a sign board (**Wp.3**). The path is way marked with green (new) and white (old) dots as we wind through two small valleys (**Wp.4**) amongst the pine-dotted slopes. Over a red earth spur, our trail drops down to cross a dirt road (**Wp.5, 12M**). Turning left, we stroll up the dirt road to pass a restored cottage (**Wp.6**) and come up to a large threshing circle on the lip of the *barranco* (**Wp.7**) with stunning views. We continue along the dirt road until it swings left (**Wp.8**) and then walk up to the remains of a sign board and a 'pa' sign (**Wp.9, 20M**).

The temptation is to continue up the broad ridge for the views from its head, but hidden beside the "pa" sign we take a stone-laid donkey trail which drops into the *barranco*. This amazing path winds down through a gateway (**Wp.10**) into a pocket of stunning flora; pruning shears are useful to keep the narrow path open through the vigorous vegetation. Our narrow path levels out to run beneath the outcrop's sheer cliffs, with the *barranco* plummeting down on our right, and careful footwork is needed on the narrower sections. From beneath the cliffs our path climbs up to bring us onto a saddle of sand-gold rock between the outcrop and **Roque Abinque**; more stunning views (**Wp.11, 35M**).

On the east of the saddle a small path, marked by cairns, runs along above the **Barranco del Agua**. Ahead **Playa de las Américas** is framed by the *barranco* walls, and a rock 'finger' indicates our destination. If you continue on the main path at a path junction (**Wp.12**), it will take you up to a stone corral perched on the ridge between the *barrancos*. We take the lower path which swings right above a water canal (**Wp.13**) and then crosses the canal (**Wp.14, 42M**) just before an eroded section (**Wp.15**) where we need to edge along the canal.

Our narrow path brings us onto the saddle by the rock 'finger' outcrop (**Wp.16**) before we go down to the right for stunning views from a ledge in the *barranco* wall (**Wp.17, 50M**) where a section of canal makes a comfortable seat in this most orogenic of landscapes. Take a picnic break on this mountain ledge drinking in one of Tenerife's most spectacular views.

Our route has been on an old, and largely forgotten, donkey trail which runs down to **Adeje**, but just beyond our finish point serious erosion starts and the trail is officially regarded as 'muy abandonado' which is unfortunate as, potentially, it would have been one of Tenerife's most stunning descents. We return by the same route.

Wow! Spectacular

11. QUEEN OF THE SOUTH

This walk certainly lives up to its 'royal' title. We start at the **Ifonche** junction and set out on a journey through a 'timescape' of agricultural settlements, pine forests, incredible *barrancos* and valleys, to emerge at the best *mirador* view in the south. The final descent of 650 metres altitude into **Adeje** is unfortunately more memorable for the rough track than the views - good footwear is essential - but don't let this put you off this grand walk.

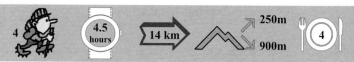

| 4 | 4.5 hours | 14 km | | 250m / 900m | 4 |

To reach our start point we take the bus (N°s 342, 482) up to the **Ifonche** junction on the outskirts of **La Escalona** and walk up the road before dropping down to cross the **Barranco de Funes**. A stiff climb then brings us up onto the **Ifonche** plateau, followed by gentle strolling along the road passing two bars, the tiny church and the **El Refugio** turning, before going down into the **Barranco del Rey**. A further stiff climb then brings us up to the end of the tarmac at **Bar El Dornajo** (unlikely to be open before 13.00) in **Ifonche** (**Wp.1, 60M**).

An alternative, but much tougher, start can be made from **Arona** by walking up the **Vilaflor** road to the **Granja Arona** where we take the dirt road down to the *embalse* featured in our 'Fantasia' route. From the *embalse* you can take either the 'Fantasia' return route to **Ifonche** (**90M**) or the reverse of 'Fantasia' downward route, much more scenic but tougher and longer (**120M**).

At **Bar El Dornajo** (**Wp.1, 0M**) our 'Fantasia' route turns left, but today we follow the start of 'Wow! Spectacular' route (**Wps.2, 3 & 4**), until we come down to the dirt road in the bottom of the valley (**Wp.5, 12M**) where we head straight across the dirt road.

Our narrow walking trail climbs up from the valley floor and turns inland to steadily ascend the ridge. A steady ascent on the rough path brings us up to a bowl where terraces have been built amongst the pines, or perhaps where pines have colonised former agricultural terraces. We come to the end of a terrace wall, the trail continuing below the wall and climbing gently to bring us to the edge of the pine forest (**Wp.6, 17M**).

A clear trail leads into the forest, signed by a white arrow on a boulder, going gently uphill beneath the trees. We come up to a junction where we take the narrower needle-covered trail, following a white arrow, to climb steeply up towards the top of the ridge on our left. There are plenty of white arrow way marks to keep us on the path as we climb through a series of bends (**Wp.7**) to the crest of the ridge. On the ridge, large arrows made of rocks point in both directions along the path. A small cairn marks the continuation of the path and we go gently downhill. On our left we look down into the canyon of **Barranco del Infierno** and catch glimpses of the sea through the pines. Our trail runs downhill, with occasional climbs, along the wall of this magnificent canyon 250 metres above the route of our 'Barranco del Infierno' walk.

We walk below sheer cliffs, the long drop into the canyon on our left as we progress towards the head of the *barranco*. The path drops steeply, and we need to take care not to slip on the pine needle-covered trail, before levelling out to run below an impressive promontory. Sounds of running water and the waterfall come up from the canyon's depths, and passing through a rock channel, we go downhill to round a pocket in the canyon wall. The path runs down out of the pocket to round a promontory by a mature Canarian pine; from here we enjoy *mirador* views down into the sheer-sided *barranco*.

After the viewing point we come to a junction of paths (**Wp.8, 28M**). We take the right hand path, signed **TS3**, to climb steeply up the narrow trail along the *barranco* wall. The path zigzags up to come under cliffs as we continue through a rock channel, and then more cliffs before the ascent eases. We now stroll along to an area where the tumbled boulders of a huge rock slide cover the steep slopes. Our trail cuts through the sea of boulders to drop steeply down until we come out onto the floor of the canyon (**Wp.9, 38M**), now above the **Barranco del Infierno** and technically on the floor of **Barranco de la Fuente**.

Picking our way over the grey boulders, we come back onto the continuation of our route and start climbing up the western wall of the canyon.

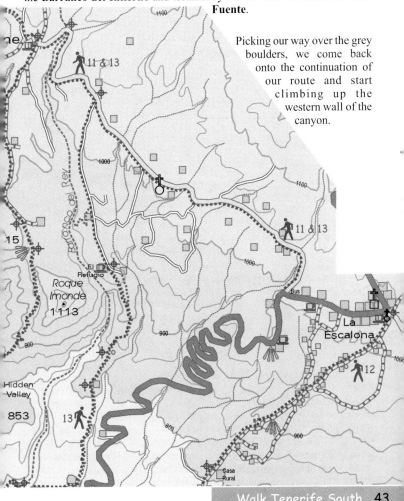

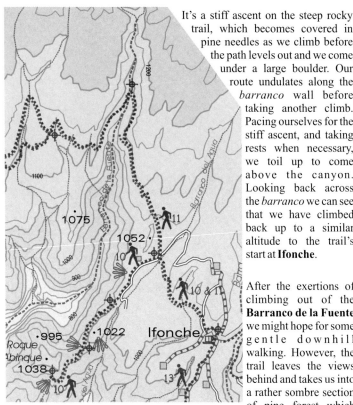

It's a stiff ascent on the steep rocky trail, which becomes covered in pine needles as we climb before the path levels out and we come under a large boulder. Our route undulates along the *barranco* wall before taking another climb. Pacing ourselves for the stiff ascent, and taking rests when necessary, we toil up to come above the canyon. Looking back across the *barranco* we can see that we have climbed back up to a similar altitude to the trail's start at **Ifonche**.

After the exertions of climbing out of the **Barranco de la Fuente** we might hope for some gentle downhill walking. However, the trail leaves the views behind and takes us into a rather sombre section of pine forest which clothes a land of valleys and sharp-sided *barrancos*. Our trail is clearly way marked with white dots and arrows, as we cross gentle valleys (**Wp.11**) and two sharp-sided *barrancos* (**Wps.12 & 13**) beneath the shade of the silent forest. A few cistus 'rock rose' bushes relieve the tedium of this brown needle-covered ground. As the valleys become shallower we need to pay careful attention to the route's way marking. Coming up a gentle slope we approach a pair of pines where the main path turns right (**Wp.14, 56M**); looking to our right we can see an arrow twenty metres up the gentle slope. Although this appears as a major junction both paths have the same destination, the right hand path crossing **Barranco Chavon** at **Wp.15** while the straight-on path crosses the steep **Barranco Chavon** at **Wp.16** and after climbing out of the *barranco*, runs on through the pines to a multi-junction of paths (**Wp.17, 72M**) where we join the upper crossing route.

From the rejoining of the trails the forest steadily changes, becoming more colourful as the trail leads us through a series of shallow valleys (**Wps.18, 19 & 20**) to come to a junction (**Wp.21, 88M**) at the edge of the forest. Ahead the main trail leads up onto an area of clear rock with a signboard (**Wp.22**), the main route to **Taucho**. Following the left hand trail we come onto bare rock to find a hand-carved rock water channel. Boots have worn faint trails across the rock for us to parallel the small water channel. Away on our right we look over a *barranco* to the outlying houses of **Taucho** village, as our path continues going gently downhill to an area of red earth marked by a cairn. If you go over

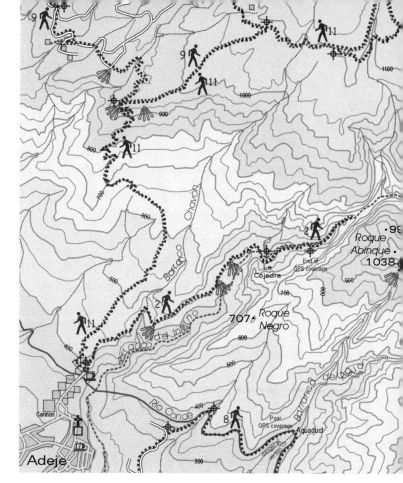

to your left at this point you will find the water channel again, and a spectacular view down over **Adeje** from the edge of the *cumbre*. This path swings right to run along below a low ridge and becomes very water-eroded before it meets a path (**Wp.23**) and then swings left onto the donkey trail at **Lomo de las Lajas (Wp.24, 107M)** with its superb panoramic views.

The descent from **Lomo de las Lajas** starts well on a stone-laid donkey trail descending below orange cliffs. However, at the end of this short section the trail deteriorates into a rocky, boulder strewn, path which has suffered from water erosion. For an alternative finish in **Taucho** see our 'Taucho Tour' route. It's a long, tortuous, winding route down the mountainside requiring continuous concentration on what must be the roughest trail on the island - well cushioned footwear is absolutely essential. Having to concentrate on every footfall doesn't allow much opportunity to look at the scenery, and makes the last hour of the walk seem even longer. Eventually the downward toil finishes when we meet the tarmac (**Wp.25**) and stroll down the smooth surface to the start of the **Barranco del Infierno** walk (**Wp.26, 197M**) at **Otello's** restaurant, although if it is Tuesday you will need to continue down into **Adeje** for refreshment, and buses back to the resorts.

12. WALKERS WHO LUNCH

Our downhill power walk descends from 1,050 metres altitude by a little-known route through rural countryside, taking in the county town of **Arona**. Finishing at 400 metres altitude in **Valle San Lorenzo** after descending through the impressive views seen at the start in **La Escalona**. We make no apologies for this walk being mostly on smooth tarmac, nor that it is all downhill and finishes at one of Tenerife's famous restaurants (but not expensive!) - the marvellous panoramic views and flora, plus an unusual garden fully justify this as a walking route.

This walk is best saved for a relaxing day after you have completed all other routes. Take a gentle, scenic bus ride up to La Escalona (342 **Mount Teide** bus or 482 **Vilaflor** bus) and enjoy our downhill route finishing with a 'Power Lunch'.

In **La Escalona** the main road turns sharp left around the church square, and three other roads form a junction with the main road. Select the smallest road beside **Bar La Curva (Wp.1, 0M)**; the **San Miguel TF-565** road is on our the left. Leaving the junction, we follow the tiny road past the local *correos* (post office) and round to the right past a small *ermita* to overlook our downhill route. Below us a vista of mountain slopes and peaks roll away to the coastal plain. The road, once the main donkey trail down to the county town of **Arona**, pays lip service to vehicles with a thin covering of tarmac, but few drivers know of or use this unmapped road. It is all downhill as the road drops steeply between farms, some working, others abandoned, and modern villas. Tarmac tracks lead off our narrow tarmac route, and terraces line both sides of the route, citrus groves and vines alternating with wild cacti, aloes, yuccas and endemic species.

Over on our right mounts **Conde** and **Imonde** dominate the landscape as we look down on the main road climbing up the valley. Downhill through this bucolic landscape we pass old and new houses, this little route is becoming a popular place to build your large villa in the country, including the *Casa Rural* **Correa del Almendro (Wp.2)**, until we come to where the *camino rural* swings sharp left (**Wp.3**). Ahead, we go down a section of the old stone-laid donkey trail, passing an old farmhouse before rejoining the tarmac (**Wp.4**). A few metres on we come to a cross and thoughtfully placed bench seat (**Wp.5**) if you would like a relaxed break at this point. The road continues steeply down, becomes **Calle San Antonio** and literally drops us down into the town square of **Arona (Wp.6, 38M)**.

On this first section we have descended 400 metres at an average slope of one in ten - a very good reason for choosing to walk the route downhill. At **Arona** there are bars off the town square for refreshment. Should you choose to finish walking here and return to the resort, continue straight over the town square down to the bus terminus and the 480 bus will take you to **Los Cristianos**.

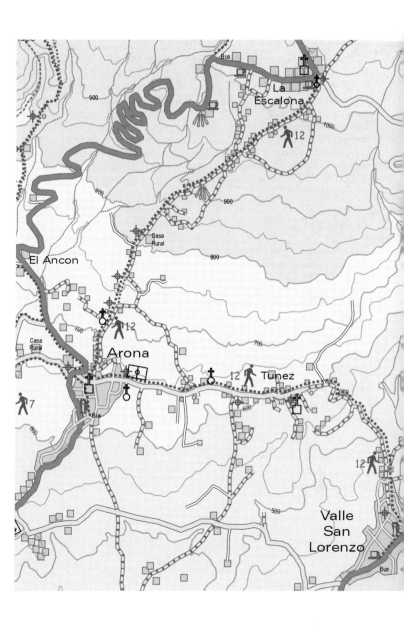

The second stage of our walk takes us out of **Arona** on the **Túnez** road (turn left at the end of **Calle San Antonio**) past the **RACE** office. In contrast to our steep descent into **Arona,** the **Túnez** road undulates around the 600 metre contour, even going uphill to pass the football stadium (**L**) and chapel (**R**) (**Wp.7**), before running along between a variety of homes ranging from simple habitations to Fort Knox style villas. One view not to be missed is after we pass a *camino rural* off to our right (**Wp.8**) an unusual garden starts on our right, modern sculptures and stonework mixing with a Japanese style in a most pleasing aspect. Passing the top of the property - note the hatchet and block - we find this most impressive of gardens is simply named number 66. The next house, **La Esperanza**, was also briefly famous in the News of the World but is now better known for the large blue thing in its garden. Strolling on we pass **Túnez** church on our right (**Wp.9**) and head out into the country. Our road has narrowed, and when it swings right by a house and crosses a water canal, we start dropping down into the valley behind **Valle San Lorenzo**. Gentle strolling, with a few skittery steep sections, bring us down to the houses of the town and a Y-junction (**Wp.10**) where we go left. Down the narrow street we swing left and right to drop onto the main road (**Wp.11**) and go right. **Valle San Lorenzo** is in a state of parking gridlock, much easier to walk in and bus out, as we struggle (**SW**) past the petrol station to arrive at our destination (**Wp.12, 87M**); **Cafeteria Paraiso**.

Behind the simple exterior is one of the most popular eating places in the south of Tenerife with an extensive menu, good service and good prices (reservations essential in the evenings). One skinflint expat. describes this establishment as expensive, but all thinking people will recognise the top quality and excellent value that makes it so popular, though this may mean that we have to wait for a table. As a walker you will empathise with the understated sporting excellence of Cafeteria Paraiso; the *parapente* pilots you may have seen landing on the town outskirts are regulars here. Head honcho, Alejandro, is a well respected triathalon competitor (his younger brother is a professional footballer), Clara is a former Gran Canaria triathalon champion, and Toño (the owner) is famous for his Fiat-Abarth car racing; if you have some free time, ask him about his cars! Also the 416 bus stop is just outside for the service down to **Los Cristianos**.

13. FANTASIA

We make no apologies for borrowing the famous Disney film title to describe this spectacular walk. Our route takes us from scene to scene, almost as if the landscape is being transformed around us. Whether it is the mountains, spectacular views, hidden valley, verdant plant life, or the unusual geology which you find most breathtaking, the sum of all these parts is pure 'Fantasia' - truly one of the south's most spectacular walks. Designed as a circular walk for car drivers, this route can be made linear to **Arona** or **Vento** if you are using the TITSA bus service; reduce exertion rating to 3 walker.

4 | 3 hours | 9 km | 550m / 550m | 4

Start for bus users

We start by catching the 342 or 482 bus up to the **Ifonche** junction (**Cruce de Ifonche**) bus stop. From the junction we walk up the steep start of the **Ifonche** road to swing across the **Barranco de Funes** and climb up to the **Ifonche Plateau**. For the first hour we follow the quiet road down past **Bar Pedro** and passing the turning to **El Refugio** (**Wp.26**), before dropping into the **Barranco de Ifonche** (**Wp.28**) and a stiff climb up to **Bar El Dornajo** (**Wp.29, 3.2km**), usually open from 13.00, closed Thursdays) in **Ifonche**. If you can get a lift or taxi to **Ifonche** you can reduce the walking time by one hour.

At **El Dornajo** we turn left (**S**) to walk along the narrow road passing another tiny road going up to the left while we continue straight on. As we stroll down below a terrace wall, away on our right is an impressive farming settlement, its massive terrace walls giving the look of a fortified promontory. After running downhill, the road climbs quite steeply up to a house before levelling out to run along a ridge for us to come to a road junction with a sturdy wooden cross set in a concrete base (**Wp.1, 4km**) where a road drops down into the valley on our left.

Start for car users

Follow the same directions as for bus travellers and park near the wooden cross; often parking at **El Dornajo** is rather fraught.

Onward route

From the cross (**Wp.1, 0M**) we stroll along the ridge on the road heading towards **Roque Imonde**. On our right we pass a huge head-shaped rock outcrop, **Garcia's Nose,** as we come under the heights of **Roque de los Brezos**. Our route goes gently downhill through Canarian pines as we walk above large abandoned terraces below us on the left, undulating along below **Roque de los Brezos** to come above cultivated terraces and a farm house. Ahead is the saddle between **Roque Imonde** and **Roque de los Brezos** which is our first destination.

As the road swings left to run down to the farmhouse, look for a path (**Wp.2, 8M**) which runs below the ridge to cross the open ground and climb gently up to the saddle. If you miss the first path, look for a white marker post below the road on your right just before reaching the farmhouse. A faint trail goes down below a terrace and across to a derelict building, from which you go up over open ground to the saddle. Do not go past the farmhouse on the road as its backyard is filled with hunting dogs and a couple of guard dogs!

As we reach the saddle a spectacular view over the resort of **Playa de las Américas** welcomes our arrival. Set on the saddle is a large threshing circle (**Wp.3**) dating from the old days when the terraces stretching up the slopes of **Roque Imonde** were cultivated. From the threshing circle, we walk a few metres up the spine to find a narrow walking trail which runs around the west side of the mountain under a large rock outcrop with a green paint mark. We follow the rough trail as it traverses the steep slopes, wild plants abounding on these moist western slopes. Magnificent views are always with us on this section - remember to 'Stop to look, and look where you put your feet'. Our path runs into and out of pockets in the side of the mountain above the heads of *barrancos* down below us, undulating around promontories (**Wp.4** marks rounding the first promontory) and through pockets with an occasional steep descent. Parts of the trail suffer from water erosion and combined with the occasional loose rock surface, we carefully pick our way around the mountain.

A gentle climb as the path comes up to round a promontory on red rock, heralds a change in the nature of our route. We turn around lichen-covered rock into another pocket to pass small volcanic 'blow holes' in the rock on our left. Taking care crossing water-eroded sections of the path for two narrow sections of path (**Wp.5, 27M**), we climb out of the pocket onto a spur running down from **Roque Imonde**. **Roque del Conde** comes back into view as we reach the spur and we look down onto the gentle landscape of the **Hidden Valley** (**Wp.6**). Neat, though abandoned, terraces ring this bowl in the mountains where in spring field marigolds create a golden carpet, adding to the atmosphere. Our path runs down the promontory to turn down into the valley, the loose rock path zigzagging down the slope before running along a rock channel. Down over coloured rock, we cross an old water channel (**Wp.7**) and emerge above the valley's top terrace. Taking care not to get spiked by prickly pear, we come down to the threshing circle (**Wp.8, 40M**), set on the saddle between the rounded hills.

The **Hidden Valley** is an ideal place to take a break if you wish to explore the remains of this once self-sufficient pocket in the mountains. Several caves had been converted to agricultural use, and a stone-roofed water cistern provided a substantial water resource for the small community. You could easily spend an hour or two exploring this idyllic environment.

To leave the **Hidden Valley**, we walk up from the threshing circle in the direction of **Roque del Conde**. As we climb we come onto a faint trail which passes a pair of caves on our left as it circles a rounded ridge. After levelling out the path runs below the rounded peak on our left and above a sharp sided *barranco* on our right, before climbing gently to round the promontory. We come to a rock outcrop on our right with beautiful views across to the ridges of **Roque de los Brezos** and down over **Adeje**. Below us, our onward route snakes through an unusual geological formation of sharp ridges towards the **Degollada de los Frailitos**. From a gnarled outcrop of rock we swing left and

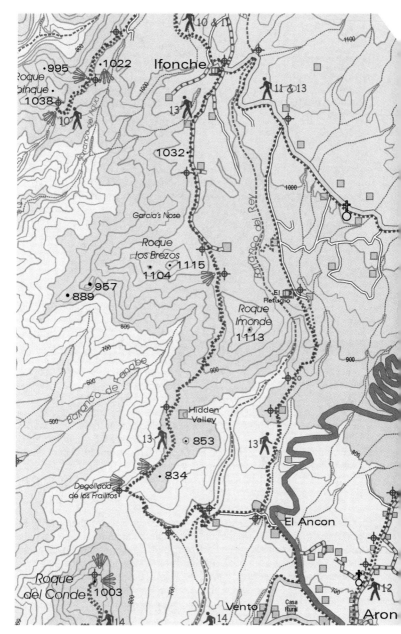

gradually drop down the gravely path between vertical plates of rock and onto the *degollada*.

We follow the faint trail towards the saddle of **Degollada de los Frailitos** to pass an outcrop of shattered rock (**Wp.9, 52M**) with views over **Adeje** to the west coast, while across from us an unusual natural rock arch tops the jagged ridge running down from **Roque de los Brezos**. Our trail runs out to the

Above Barranco del Rey with Roque Imonde in the background.

degollada (**Wp.10**), where we turn our backs on **Adeje** and head down over rock slopes with ancient abandoned terraces on our right. Occasional stone cairns mark a faint trail down to strike a broken down rock wall at the edge of the terraces, where the path becomes clearer. Keeping the wall on our right, we follow its line until the path swings left across the rock slopes to cross a small watercourse. Our trail wanders along and then zigzags (**Wp.11, 59M**) down to cross the watercourse (**Wp.12**) again.

The narrow walking trail meanders along the right hand (**S**) side of the watercourse through a wild hillside below ancient terraces. Our clear but narrow trail comes down beside the watercourse to a faint junction (**Wp.13, 65M**), where we follow the main trail over the watercourse to climb around the hillside on a clear dirt path which brings us to the lip of the **Barranco del Rey** and along to the top of an old donkey trail dropping into the *barranco* (**Wp14, 70M**). It is a steep, zigzagging, descent requiring careful footwork before emerging on the floor of the *barranco* by a "pa" sign (**Wp.15, 74M**); just the place to take a cool break in the shade (mornings) before tackling the long ascent back to **Ifonche**.

A few metres down the *barranco* we come to the restart of the *sendero*. It is onwards and upwards on the boulder-laid trail to steadily climb up through a series of zigzags, taking rests when necessary. The path levels out at an area of red earth below small cliffs, giving us *mirador* views back over a landscape untouched by man for decades. From the red earth, the path runs along the lip of the *barranco* below the cliffs (**Wp.16**) before turning left to climb up over rock and away from the *barranco* on a rough path to come alongside abandoned terraces. The tiled roof of a cottage comes into view as our route follows the edge of the terraces to pass behind the cottage (**Wp.17**). From the cottage we follow a rough donkey trail up between tumbled stone walls, passing a disused water cistern on our right, to come onto a dirt road. It's a gentle stroll along the dirt road as it starts to run downhill to come below the wall of an *embalse* (**Wp.18, 86M**).

Linear walkers should continue on the main dirt road where a rock and concrete bridge crosses the **Barranco del Ancón**. From the bridge it is a steady climb up the rough dirt road to meet the main road at the **La Granja de Arona** restaurant (open from 13.00 - but closed Tuesdays) for a ten minute stroll down the main road (watch out for the traffic) to turn left by the **Centro de Acogida de Arona** and walk down **Calle Prolongación D'Alfonso** to **Arona** town square. Another alternative is to go right at the **Vento** junction, signed **Roque del Conde**, to pick up our **Arona** to **Playa las Américas** route.

For us circular walkers we now start to pay for all that downhill as we go up a rocked-off dirt road signed to **El Refugio**. Coming up round the *embalse* we face slopes of abandoned farm land stretching up to the horizon. A rough path, well waymarked with white splodges, takes us up between the picturesque **Barranco del Ancón** and a large water channel. It is a steady, relentless ascent, which distracts from the beautiful views, to cross a metal water pipe (**Wp.19**) before coming up to a tumbled cottage (**Wp.20, 108M**). After the cottage the gradient eases for us to stroll up to a circular water tank (**Wp.21**) and cross the water channel to walk across to abandoned terraces. Now the ascent starts again as the white splodged path takes us up through the old terraces onto a steep section of the path which brings a white house into view. Before reaching the house white splodges guide us off the path (**Wp.22**) to climb up onto a really rough old rock road. It is a stiff climb up to pass the white house and come onto a dirt road with the welcoming sight of **El Refugio** ahead; a final few metres bring us up to this unique hostelry (**Wp.23, 133M**).

Suitably refreshed we head up the dirt road to pass a goat farm (**L**), and dirt road (**R**) (**Wp.24**). For the adventurous you can descend into **Barranco del Rey** on a donkey trail behind the goat farm; unfortunately the continuation on the far slope has been long abandoned leading to a lively ascent. Our choice is to continue up the dirt road, passing a dirt road off to the right (**Wp.25**), to the **Ifonche** road (**Wp.26, 149M**) to turn left and follow the tarmac. As we drop into the **Barranco del Rey** there is an intriguing dirt road off to the left (**Wp.27**) before we come down to the watercourse (**Wp.28, 159M**) where a **Vilaflor** walking route is signed off the road. A steep climb brings us up to **El Dornajo** (**Wp.29**) for the possibility of more refreshment before heading out on the narrow tarmac lane to our starting point (**Wp.1, 174M**).

14. TABLE MOUNTAIN

Roque del Conde's 1000 metres 'table top' peak dominates the coastal plain of southern Tenerife. From the top, the views are simply stupendous, rewarding the stiff climb up this impressive mountain, which will also appeal to plant enthusiasts. This route is for fit walkers who can confidently tackle the climb totalling 450 metres on rough tracks requiring good, well cushioned, walking footwear.

Our starting point is at the junction of the **Vento** road with the TF-51, just above **Arona**'s town square, where there is plenty of parking; please do not park on the narrow roads in **Vento** village. If arriving by bus, then from the **Arona** terminus walk up the street to the town square to take the **Calle Prolongación D'Alfonso** from the north-west corner of the square. Climbing up the steep street we then cross carefully over the main road to our start point by the public telephone (**Wp.1, 0M**).

We climb up from the main road to views down to the coast as the lane swings left and past **La Casa del Pintur** *casa rural* (**Wp.2**) before the lane runs down between the first houses of **Vento**. We stroll down to the religious obelisk at the T-junction (**Wp.3, 6M**) and turning left we come down to the **Roque del Conde** path (**Wp.4**) signed off to our right by house number 78.

After the tarmac we are on a well-made *sendero* which drops us down into the **Barranco de las Casas (Wp.5)**. Our trail runs up over rock to a crest and then drops us down the **Barranco del Ancón (Wp.6)**. Across the valley floor, a gentle climb brings us up to walk alongside the *barranco*, passing a path off to our left (**Wp.7**), until our trail swings right across a water channel to a junction of paths. We go straight ahead over rock to a 'pa' sign (**Wp.8**) and confront the **Barranco del Rey**. At the lip of the *barranco* wall we come onto a well-made *sendero* which zigzags steeply down towards the *barranco* floor. Stone walls, with posts mounted in them, line the *sendero* as we drop down on its rough boulder surface. After twists and turns we come onto the valley floor (**Wp.9, 22M**) just above a waterfall (when water runs down the *barranco*) with sheer cliff walls rising fifty metres up on each side of us.

Straight across the valley floor, we come onto another rough boulder *sendero*, marked by white arrows, and start climbing. We toil up the stiff climb, which gets steeper as we get higher, until a set of stone steps brings us to the top of the *barranco* wall (**Wp.10**). Ahead, **Roque del Conde** looms over us as a prominent trail goes right but we take the path to the left. Climbing up past a white arrow, our dirt path winds it way up to a gold rock slab, with views back to **Vento**, and continues on towards a crumbling cottage.

Over a small crest the path runs down past a small water cistern (**Wp.11**) the size of a bath, on our right. Above the water cistern, unseen by most walkers, is an opening in the rock. Climbing up the rock slope we find ourselves looking through the narrow opening into a large subterranean cavern. A small

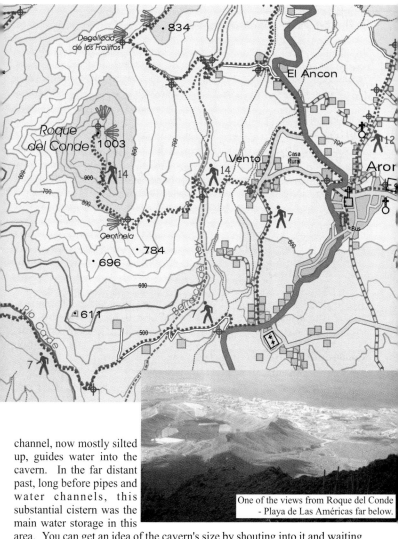

One of the views from Roque del Conde
- Playa de Las Américas far below.

channel, now mostly silted up, guides water into the cavern. In the far distant past, long before pipes and water channels, this substantial cistern was the main water storage in this area. You can get an idea of the cavern's size by shouting into it and waiting for the echo! Leaving this historical site we drop back down onto the path to continue on to the cottage (**Wp.12, 30M**).

Our trail climbs up past the north wall of the cottage. We pass two threshing circles on our left (**Wps.13 & 14**) as we continue up over the abandoned terraces to come onto a boulder-laid donkey trail (**Wp.15**) to continue straight uphill. Our trail swings left for us to head diagonally across the slope in a relentless climb towards the saddle at **Centinela**. At the end of the 'long straight', the donkey trail becomes rougher and continues upwards through a series of zigzags as we climb towards the saddle. It is a steep, relentless climb so pace yourself and take rests whenever necessary. We come onto another 'long straight' of the donkey trail and continue toiling upwards. Ahead large birds circle above the ridge, like buzzards in a western but here, only seagulls!

The donkey trail swings right for another 'long straight' pointing towards **Roque del Conde**, before swinging left for the last 'long straight' of the route.

At the end of the last 'long straight' we swing right and the donkey trail finishes for us to continue climbing on a narrow dirt path. We climb steeply up through a series of zigzags to reach the saddle at **Centinela (Wp.16, 51M)**. The path opens out into a small clear area, like an unofficial *mirador*. As we climb onto the ridge, spectacular views open up over the resort of **Playa de las Américas** over 700 metres below us.

We take a break on the *mirador* to enjoy the vistas laid out below us. East, our start point in **Arona**, can be seen 150 metres below our present position, and this difference in altitude leads us to question our next step. From the *mirador* it is a narrow, often rough, path which includes steep climbs totalling 250 metres to the top of **Roque del Conde**, and 250 metres back down to the *mirador*. If at this point you are very tired, then rest at the *mirador* before returning the same way down to **Vento** and **Arona**. Similarly, if you encounter bad weather, or if **Conde** has become cloud covered, finish at **Centinela** and return to **Arona**.

From **Centinela** a narrow path goes right (**NW**) along the ridge towards **Roque del Conde**, marked by white paint. Our route undulates along to take us across the southern face of the mountain until we swing right (**Wp.17**) for a zigzag ascent. We come above the hidden valley which lies behind **Playa de las Américas**, the head of the valley and one ridge filled with *embalses* while the floor is covered with banana plantations. The loose rock and dirt path climbs steeply to bring us up onto sheets of orange rock below ten metre high cliffs (**Wp.18**).   Going left, we continue to circle the mountain following the trail as it climbs around rock promontories. It is onwards and upwards through a series of steep climbs, the path splitting (**Wp.19**) and rejoining (**Wp.20**) just above a 'TS4' white paint marker.

A final toiling ascent brings us onto the edge of the plateau (**Wp.21, 83M**), and a surprise. On the mountain-top we find long abandoned agricultural terraces - sometime in the distant past someone used to farm this least-accessible area of land! A path, trodden down by walkers, leads across the terraces towards the mound and height marker at the official peak of **Roque del Conde**. As we approach the peak we find the large mound covered in a sea of asphodels (Asphodelus tenuifolius), a beautiful sight when in flower February - May. Pushing through the flowers we come to the height marker (**Wp.22, 88M**). **Roque del Conde** is the final mountain in the chain surrounding **Las Cañadas**, and inland is the 'turret' peak of **Roque Imonde**. Here, standing suspended high above the surrounding lands, we have awesome views over the south and west coasts - a fitting reward for the effort of the climb.

We return by the same route; there is no other way up or down; taking extreme care on the steep descent down to the *mirador*. After the *mirador* the path and donkey trail make for an easier descent, though it can be hard on the knees. The climbs out of the three *barrancos*, particularly **Barranco del Rey**, give a small reminder of our earlier efforts before we arrive back at **Arona**.

GERANIUM WALK

Tenerife's longest sea-front promenade, 'Geranium Walk', stretches from the **Costamar** apartments at the south-eastern tip of **Los Cristianos** all the way through the resorts of **Los Cristianos**, **Playa las Americas**, **Playa Fañabe** and **Costa Adeje** to the developing village of **La Caleta**.

Originally named by us in our 1988 street plans, 'Geranium Walk' was soon adopted as the official name for this coastal promenade. Since 1988, development has extended westwards, increasing the length of the promenade from 7 kilometres to its present 9.8 kilometres.

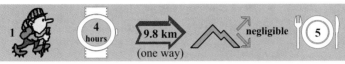

Geranium Walk contrasts with our country and mountain routes, giving you an urban experience of southern Tenerife. Dress is strictly informal, footwear is comfortable casual, and speed is not of the essence. Bars and restaurants beyond count line the route, obviating the need for supplies, and navigation is as simple as it can be. Best maps are the Street Plans included in 'Tenerife Indestructible Map' and 'Drive Tenerife Touring Map', both of which have the latest street plans, and are the only maps to include **Playa Fañabe** and **Costa Adeje**.

Finding Geranium Walk is simplicity itself. Simply walk towards the sea until you come to the pedestrian walkway. Our preference is to start at **Costamar** and finish at **La Caleta**. Few directions are needed, but at the end of **Los Cristianos** beach as you come to the fresh fish stalls, go right to walk through the tunnel to emerge alongside **Playa las Vistas**. After the seaward side of the notorious **Veronicas**, go right and follow the pavement past **Playas Troya** up to the roundabout; the bar just below the walkway makes a suitable refreshment stop with views over the frolicking sunbathers. Just past the roundabout, Geranium Walk leaves the road to run down to **Playa Bobo** before the **Bouganville** stairs bring us back up onto the headland.

At **Puerto Colón** marina, take the stairs down to circle **Playa La Pinta** before rounding the headland to **Playa Fañabe**, with the impressive **Bahía del Duque** hotel ahead of us.

Past **Playa Fañabe**, the new hotels become even more impressive before finishing at the **Costa Adeje Palace** hotel, inland of which is the **Ermita de San Sebastián**. We walk down to a new beach which we cross on a slatted walkway before coming up to the **La Caleta** road. A short stroll takes us through the new developments of **La Caleta** before turning left down a pedestrian walkway, to emerge at the seafront bar for refreshments while contemplating the return stroll.

- GPS Waypoints are provided for each route description in **Walk! Tenerife South** . The waypoint numbers in these lists correspond to the numbers quoted in each walk description, and are for the direction in which the authors describe the route.

- When inputting GPS Waypoints to your GPS receiver, do make sure that you have **set the datum to Pico las Nieves**; possibly known as Canary Islands or Islas Canarias datum on some receivers. Also see 'Navigation and GPS' (P.9) which provides more information.

- Note that not all GPS Waypoints are shown on the maps, and those that are shown are placed alongside the route rather than at the exact location.

- While we quote GPS Waypoints to 0.001 (1 metre) in practice 0.010 (10 metres) is an acceptable standard of accuracy. GPS Waypoints are extremely difficult to reproduce exactly while on a walking route, unless you spend some time at each waypoint location finding the exact position at which we were holding the GPS unit; hence the 10 metre accuracy for reproducing waypoints in the field or on the mountain.

- Two walking routes have problems with the 'mountain shadowing' effect which reduces GPS reception below three satellites:
  Walk 2, 'Barranco del Infierno' when deep into the canyon, and
  Walk 8, 'Adeje Skywalker' on the vertiginous section either side of the aqueduct crossing the Barranco del Agua.

- At all other times on **Walk! Tenerife South** routes, you will have good GPS reception with four or more satellites in view, even in the pine forest.

1. LIFE IN THE RAW		
Wp	N	W
1	28 06.009	16 45.207
2	28 06.137	16 45.319
3	28 06.178	16 45.336
4	28 06.264	16 45.274
5	28 06.248	16 45.391
6	28 06.259	16 45.502
7	28 06.273	16 45.508
8	28 06.405	16 45.489
9	28 06.514	16 45.585
10	28 06.532	16 45.635
11	28 06.547	16 45.645
12	28 06.551	16 45.698
13	28 06.565	16 45.751
14	28 06.583	16 45.770
15	28 06.690	16 45.704
16	28 06.693	16 45.754
17	28 06.834	16 45.755
18	28 06.846	16 45.746
19	28 06.893	16 45.765
20	28 06.875	16 45.859
21	28 06.846	16 45.849
22	28 06.796	16 45.917
23	28 06.708	16 45.954
24	28 06.606	16 45.978
25	28 06.535	16 45.996
26	28 06.550	16 45.919
27	28 06.442	16 45.522
28	28 06.032	16 45.451
29	28 06.003	16 45.440
30	28 06.062	16 45.366

2. BARRANCO DEL INFIERNO		
Wp	N	W
1	28 07.491	16 43.316
2	28 07.630	16 43.107
3	28 07.722	16 43.053
4	28 07.648	16 43.032
5	28 07.735	16 42.883
6	28 07.818	16 42.749
7	28 07.735	16 42.696
8	28 07.906	16 42.676
9	28 07.917	16 42.617
10	28 07.902	16 42.532
11	28 07.945	16 42.433
12	28 07.945	16 42.405
13	28 07.958	16 42.354

3. BARREN GRANDEUR

Wp	N	W
1	28 02.596	16 42.471
2	28 02.380	16 42.410
3	28 02.430	16 42.297
4	28 02.428	16 42.164
5	28 02.414	16 42.183
6	28 02.324	16 42.202
7	28 02.286	16 42.330
8	28 02.181	16 42.392
9	28 02.070	16 42.315
10	28 01.936	16 42.263
11	28 01.927	16 42.258
12	28 01.853	16 42.223
13	28 01.761	16 42.153
14	28 01.765	16 42.135
15	28 01.706	16 42.195
16	28 01.674	16 42.176
17	28 01.241	16 42.230
18	28 01.193	16 42.233
19	28 01.040	16 42.266
20	28 00.953	16 42.248
21	28 00.918	16 42.244
22	28 00.875	16 42.219
23	28 00.393	16 42.167
24	28 00.185	16 41.951
25	28 00.214	16 41.889
26	28 00.257	16 41.730
27	28 00.213	16 41.688
28	28 00.144	16 41.604
29	28 00.015	16 41.527
30	27 59.985	16 41.553
31	28 00.358	16 41.697
32	28 00.398	16 41.748
33	28 00.469	16 41.774
34	28 00.518	16 41.782
35	28 00.656	16 41.711
36	28 00.761	16 41.718
37	28 00.900	16 41.645
38	28 00.882	16 41.596
39	28 01.392	16 41.328
40	28 01.720	16 41.096
41	28 01.945	16 41.258
42	28 01.924	16 41.367
43	28 01.957	16 41.430
44	28 02.137	16 41.562
45	28 02.155	16 41.713
46	28 02.344	16 41.983
47	28 02.404	16 42.012

3. ALTERNATIVE FINISH - BARREN GRANDEUR

Wp	N	W
1	28 00.005	16 41.525
2	27 59.869	16 41.160
3	27 59.855	16 40.813
4	27 59.885	16 40.538
5	27 00.044	16 40.456
6	27 00.184	16 40.356
7	27 00.255	16 39.917
8	27 00.320	16 39.949
9	27 00.342	16 39.919
10	28 00.450	16 39.632
11	28 00.332	16 39.107
12	28 00.535	16 39.076
13	28 00.613	16 38.703
14	28 00.576	16 38.367

4. MOUNT GUAZA

Wp	N	W
1	28 02.514	16 42.251
2	28 02.435	16 42.299
3	28 02.429	16 42.170
4	28 02.465	16 42.096
5	28 02.450	16 42.059
6	28 02.436	16 42.044
7	28 02.403	16 42.011
8	28 02.380	16 41.960
9	28 02.328	16 41.861
10	28 02.314	16 41.828
11	28 02.460	16 41.724
12	28 02.517	16 41.673
13	28 02.552	16 41.586
14	28 02.844	16 41.338
15	28 02.892	16 41.315
16	28 02.994	16 41.343
17	28 02.063	16 41.576
18	28 02.940	16 41.633
19	28 02.895	16 41.651

5. COASTAL ESCAPISM

Wp	N	W
1A	28 00.595	16 38.222
2A	28 00.684	16 38.055
3A	28 00.672	16 37.945
4A	28 00.663	16 37.907
5A	28 00.666	16 37.859
1	28 00.468	16 38.240
2	28 00.472	16 38.129
3	28 00.490	16 37.966
4	28 00.496	16 37.953
5	28 00.482	16 37.886
6	28 00.491	16 37.846
7	28 00.643	16 37.819
8	28 00.675	16 37.823
9	28 00.774	16 37.704
10	28 00.825	16 37.676
11	28 00.937	16 37.522
12	28 01.069	16 37.198
13	28 01.069	16 37.100
14	28 01.072	16 37.084
15	28 01.056	16 37.023
16	28 01.109	16 36.961
17	28 01.133	16 36.912
18	28 01.258	16 36.546
19	28 01.314	16 36.471
20	28 01.323	16 36.383
21	28 01.351	16 36.258
22	28 01.482	16 36.314
23	28 01.523	16 36.182
24	28 01.501	16 36.080
25	28 01.537	16 35.900
26	28 01.592	16 35.834
27	28 01.628	16 35.715
28	28 01.702	16 35.596

6. PICOS LAS AMÉRICAS
(Town section)

Wp	N	W
1	28 04.536	16 43.728
2	28 04.552	16 43.648
3	28 04.542	16 43.612
4	28 04.540	16 43.510
5	28 04.549	16 43.452
6	28 04.542	16 43.377
7	28 04.558	16 43.329
8	28 04.621	16 43.234
9	28 04.590	16 43.216
10	28 04.813	16 43.132
11	28 04.904	16 43.116
12	28 04.925	16 43.113

(Picos section)

Wp	N	W
1	28 04.929	16 43.108
2	28 05.122	16 43.066
3	28 05.152	16 43.008
4	28 05.209	16 42.970
5	28 05.218	16 42.954
6	28 05.256	16 42.874
7	28 05.293	16 42.560
8	28 05.293	16 42.533
11	28 05.361	16 42.466
13	28 05.452	16 42.368
14	28 05.489	16 42.326

7. DOWN TO TOWN

Wp	N	W
1	28 05.817	16 40.775
2	28 05.937	16 40.730
3	28 05.985	16 40.849
4	28 06.015	16 41.135
5	28 05.984	16 41.159
6	28 05.841	16 41.113
7	28 05.613	16 41.154
8	28 05.467	16 41.153
9	28 05.452	16 41.247
10	28 05.434	16 41.287
11	28 05.509	16 41.271
12	28 05.457	16 41.452
13	28 05.468	16 41.510
14	28 05.417	16 41.589
15	28 05.358	16 41.722
16	28 05.247	16 41.855
17	28 05.333	16 41.977
18	28 05.502	16 42.129
19	28 05.511	16 42.237
20	28 05.492	16 42.324

8. ADEJE SKYWALKER

Wp	N	W
1	28 06.896	16 43.536
2	28 07.035	16 43.262
3	28 06.994	16 43.219
4	28 06.925	16 43.237
5	28 07.119	16 43.068
6	28 07.237	16 42.989
7	28 07.287	16 42.923
8	28 07.322	16 42.837
9	28 07.342	16 42.813
10	28 07.347	16 42.787
11	28 07.287	16 42.658
12	28 07.198	16 42.645
13	28 07.275	16 42.436
14	28 07.037	16 42.496
15	28 07.005	16 42.570
16	28 06.875	16 42.784
17	28 06.691	16 42.826
18	28 06.667	16 42.886
19	28 06.552	16 42.765
20	28 06.674	16 42.550
21	28 06.728	16 42.419
22	28 06.673	16 42.300
23	28 06.624	16 42.302
24	28 06.600	16 42.183
25	28 06.547	16 42.234
26	28 06.478	16 42.324
27	28 06.372	16 42.369
28	28 06.255	16 42.411
29	28 06.202	16 42.431
30	28 06.057	16 42.544

Wp	N	W
31	28 06.022	16 42.462
32	28 05.886	16 42.467
33	28 05.872	16 42.504
34	28 05.816	16 42.709
35	28 05.913	16 42.823
36	28 05.915	16 42.926
37	28 05.743	16 43.126
38	28 05.664	16 43.258
39	28 05.671	16 43.332
40	28 05.635	16 43.427

9. TAUCHO TOUR

Wp	N	W
1	28 08.902	16 43.513
2	28 08.875	16 43.496
3	28 08.837	16 43.491
4	28 08.769	16 43.453
5	28 08.701	16 43.378
6	28 08.671	16 43.406
7	28 08.658	16 43.368
8	28 08.652	16 43.297
9	28 08.643	16 43.272
10	28 08.611	16 43.267
11	28 08.571	16 43.222
12	28 08.607	16 43.098
13	28 08.499	16 43.112
14	28 08.457	16 43.177
15	28 08.479	16 42.988
16	28 08.611	16 42.819
17	28 08.718	16 42.550
18	28 08.726	16 42.610
19	28 08.779	16 42.651
20	28 08.806	16 42.694
21	28 08.826	16 42.745
22	28 08.866	16 42.867
23	28 08.896	16 42.966
24	28 08.878	16 43.101
25	28 08.907	16 43.177
26	28 08.974	16 43.235
27	28 08.991	16 43.272
28	28 09.055	16 43.318
29	28 09.050	16 43.342
30	28 08.997	16 43.438
31	28 08.963	16 43.472

10. WOW! SPECTACULAR

Wp	N	W
1	28 08.014	16 41.289
2	28 08.032	16 41.340
3	28 08.076	16 41.354
4	28 08.134	16 41.470
5	28 08.278	16 41.526
6	28 08.258	16 41.608
7	28 08.232	16 41.651
8	28 08.136	16 41.698

Wp	N	W
9	28 08.119	16 41.709
10	28 08.096	16 41.749
11	28 07.966	16 41.858
12	28 07.945	16 41.856
13	28 07.916	16 41.877
14	28 07.907	16 41.906
15	28 07.886	16 41.921
16	28 07.841	16 41.931
17	28 07.852	16 41.970

11. QUEEN OF THE SOUTH

Wp	N	W
1	28 08.014	16 41.289
2	28 08.032	16 41.340
3	28 08.076	16 41.354
4	28 08.134	16 41.470
5	28 08.278	16 41.526
6	28 08.424	16 41.540
7	28 08.512	16 41.572
8	28 08.685	16 41.689
9	28 08.856	16 41.636
10	28 08.670	16 41.790
11	28 08.696	16 41.805
12	28 08.707	16 41.889
13	28 08.775	16 41.956
14	28 08.744	16 41.994
15	28 08.841	16 42.072
16	28 08.696	16 42.100
17	28 08.644	16 42.220
18	28 08.665	16 42.314
19	28 08.679	16 42.384
20	28 08.710	16 42.518
21	28 08.723	16 42.546
22	28 08.727	16 42.609
23	28 08.462	16 43.170
24	28 08.437	16 43.175
25	28 07.525	16 43.363
26	28 07.499	16 43.323

12. WALKERS WHO LUNCH

Wp	N	W
1	28 07.029	16 39.812
2	28 06.468	16 40.539
3	28 06.326	16 40.617
4	28 06.218	16 40.641
5	28 06.142	16 40.697
6	28 05.942	16 40.737
7	28 05.944	16 40.597
8	28 05.895	16 40.155
9	28 05.890	16 39.900
10	28 05.494	16 39.505
11	28 05.393	16 39.428
12	28 05.311	16 39.534

13. FANTASIA

Wp	N	W
1	28 07.642	16 41.388
2	28 07.371	16 41.333
3	28 07.242	16 41.300
4	28 07.105	16 41.294
5	28 06.995	16 41.324
6	28 06.961	16 41.366
7	28 06.853	16 41.472
8	28 06.779	16 41.496
9	28 06.541	16 41.621
10	28 06.501	16 41.684
11	28 06.437	16 41.606
12	28 06.429	16 41.609
13	28 06.370	16 41.510
14	28 06.444	16 41.384
15	28 06.412	16 41.366
16	28 06.364	16 41.373
17	28 06.399	16 41.318
18	28 06.415	16 41.139
19	28 06.520	16 41.079
20	28 06.792	16 41.045
21	28 06.901	16 40.973
22	28 07.077	16 40.902
23	28 07.207	16 40.984
24	28 07.351	16 41.055
25	28 07.438	16 41.066
26	28 07.810	16 41.041
27	28 07.870	16 41.210
28	28 08.054	16 41.154
29	28 08.017	16 41.295

14. TABLE MOUNTAIN

Wp	N	W
1	28 05.982	16 40.836
2	28 06.036	16 40.986
3	28 06.005	16 41.124
4	28 05.976	16 41.147
5	28 05.982	16 41.208
6	28 06.017	16 41.271
7	28 05.970	16 41.291
8	28 05.958	16 41.323
9	28 05.952	16 41.364
10	28 05.973	16 41.391
11	28 05.912	16 41.411
12	28 05.889	16 41.421
13	28 05.889	16 41.447
14	28 05.898	16 41.465
15	28 05.899	16 41.505
16	28 05.848	16 41.700
17	28 05.937	16 41.802
18	28 05.962	16 41.768
19	28 06.037	16 41.783
20	28 06.057	16 41.784
21	28 06.066	16 41.793
22	28 06.173	16 41.801

- Bus times may change, so we advise you to collect the latest timetable from a TITSA bus station or Tourist Office.
- We include details only of those bus routes useful for getting to and from the walks in this book.
- **Bold text** indicates places on or near our walking routes.
- A 'Bono' bus ticket for 12 or 30 euros gives you reduced fares on any route, and is worthwhile if you intend using the bus service several times.
- Details of bus services can be found on www.titsa.com

112
SANTA CRUZ - ARONA
Santa Cruz - southern motorway - junctions of Caletillas - Candelaria - Güimar - Arico - Chimiche - Granadilla - and San Miguel - **Las Galletas** - **Guaza** junction - Buzanada junction - **Valle San Lorenzo** - **Arona**

SANTA CRUZ	ARONA
11.10	05.25
19.10	13.00
(Saturdays, Sundays, fiestas)	
11.30	5.25
19.45	14.00

342
PLAYA DE LAS AMÉRICAS - EL PORTILLO
Playa de las Américas - **Los Cristianos** - **Arona** - **La Escalona** - Vilaflor - Parador de Turismo - Las Cañadas del Teide - El Portillo

PLAYA DE LAS AMÉRICAS	EL PORTILLO
09.15 (A)	15.15 (B)

(A) Leaves Torviscas 15 min. before this time, and at 09.30 from Los Cristianos
(B) Leaves from the cable car at 15.40, and from the Parador at 16.00

343
PUERTO DE LA CRUZ - PLAYA DE LAS AMÉRICAS
Puerto de la Cruz - El Botánico - northern motorway - southern motorway - **Los Cristianos** - **Playa de las Américas**

PUERTO DE LA CRUZ	PLAYA DE LAS AMÉRICAS (A)
09.00	09.00
11.10	11.30
15.20	15.30
17.35	17.45

(A) Leaves Torviscas 15 min before theses times

416
GRANADILLA - GUÍA DE ISORA
Granadilla - San Miguel - **Valle San Lorenzo** - La Camella - Cabo Blanco - Buzanada junction - **Los Cristianos** - Avda. del Ferry - **Playa de las Américas** - Torviscas - Tijoco junction - Tejina de Guía - Guía de Isora

GRANADILLA		GUÍA DE ISORA	
05.30		05.30	
05.45	(A)	06.30	
06.00		07.00	
06.30		07.25	
07.00		08.00	
07.30		08.25	
08.00		09.00	
08.30		09.45	
09.05		10.15	
09.35		10.45	
10.10		11.05	
10.40		11.35	
11.10		12.05	
11.40		12.35	
12.10		13.05	
12.40		13.30	
13.00	(C)	14.00	(A)
13.30		14.30	
14.00		15.30	
14.30		15.35	(C)
15.00		16.00	
15.30		16.30	
16.30		17.15	
16.50	(A)	17.45	
17.05		18.05	
17.45		18.45	
18.15		19.15	
18.45		19.45	
19.10		20.45	
19.40		20.40	
20.15		21.00	(C)
20.40	(C)	22.00	
21.00		22.45	(A)
00.35	(D)		
(Sat, Sun, fiestas)			
05.30		05.30	
05.45	(A)	06.30	
06.30		07.15	
07.30		08.25	
08.30	(B)	09.45	
09.35		10.45	(B)
10.40		11.35	
11.40		12.35	
12.40		13.30	
13.30		14.30	
14.30	(B)	15.30	
15.30		16.30	(B)
16.30		17.45	
17.45		18.45	

18.45   19.45
19.40   20.40
20.40 (C) 22.10 (C)
21.20 (A)
00.35 (D)

(A) From and to Los Cristianos - Guía de Isora
(B) Sat, Sun & fiestas from and to La Caleta
(C) Only as far as Playa de las Américas
(D) Los Cristianos - Adeje

441

LOS CRISTIANOS - LA CALETA

Los Cristianos - Avda. del Ferry - **Playa de las Américas** - Torviscas - Fañabe - **La Caleta**

LOS CRISTIANOS		LA CALETA	
06.50		07.30	
08.10		08.50	
09.00	(A,B)	09.45	(A)
09.55		10.30	
11.15		12.00	
12.55		13.40	
14.55		15.40	
15.30	(A)	16.45	(A)
16.30		17.20	
18.00		18.45	
19.55		20.40	

(A) Via Adeje
(B) Leaves from Playa de las Américas

442

PLAYA DE LAS AMÉRICAS - VALLE SAN LORENZO

Playa de las Américas - Avda. del Ferry - **Los Cristianos** - Chayofa - La Camella - Cabo Blanco - Buzanada - **Valle San Lorenzo** (*not Sat, Sun or fiestas*)

PLAYA DE LAS AMÉRICAS		VALLE SAN LORENZO	
08.00	(A)	08.30	(B)
09.30	(B)	10.30	(B)
14.30	(B)	15.30	(B,C)
16.30	(B,C)	17.30	(B,C)

(A) Playa de las Américas bus station - Chayofa - La Camella - Valle San Lorenzo
(B) Via Buzanada
(C) Via Centro de Salud El Mojón

450

PLAYA DE LAS AMÉRICAS - SAN ISIDRO

Playa de las Américas (bus station) - Avda. del Ferry - **Los Cristianos** - southern motorway - San Miguel junction - Reina Sofia airport junction - Granadilla junction - San Isidro (*not Sat, Sun or fiestas*)

PLAYA DE LAS AMÉRICAS	SAN ISIDRO
07.45	06.45
08.45	07.45
09.45	08.45
to	09.45
19.45	10.45
every 2 hours	to
	20.45
	every 2 hours

467

PLAYA DE LAS AMÉRICAS - LAS GALLETAS

Playa de las Américas - Avda. del Ferry - **Los Cristianos** - **Las Galletas**

PLAYA DE LAS AMÉRICAS	LAS GALLETAS
06.40	06.20
07.00	06.35
08.00	07.05
09.00	07.45
10.00	to
to	13.05
22.00	every 30/40 mins
every 30/40 mins	14.05
22.50	to
23.15	19.05
23.50	every 30/40 mins
00.15	19.40
	to
	22.40

470

GRANADILLA - PLAYA DE LAS AMÉRICAS

Playa de las Américas - Avda. del Ferry - **Los Crisitanos** - **Las Galletas** - **Golf del Sur** - **Los Abrigos** - El Médano - San Isidro - Granadilla

GRANADILLA		PLAYA DE LAS AMÉRICAS	
06.00	(A)	06.45	(A)
07.00		07.30	
07.05		to	
08.30	(A)	13.30	(A)
09.30		every 60 mins	
10.35		14.30	
11.30		15.30	
12.30		16.30	
13.30		to	
14.30	(A)	19.30	
to		every 60 mins	
17.30		20.40	
every 60 mins			
18.40			
19.30	(A)		
20.30			

(A) Does not stop at Golf del Sur

473

LAS GALLETAS - LOS GIGANTES

Las Galletas - **Los Cristianos** - Avda. del Ferry - **Playa de las Américas** - Torviscas - **Adeje** - Armeñime - Playa San Juan - Playa la Arena - Puerto Santiago - **Los Gigantes**

LAS GALLETAS		LOS GIGANTES	
05.25	(B)	06.15	
05.45	(B)	06.45	
06.00	(A)	07.15	(D)
06.15		07.45	
06.40		08.15	
06.45		08.45	
07.15		09.05	(C)
07.45		09.15	
08.10		09.25	(C)

to	09.45
19.45	10.05 (C)
every 20 mins	10.15
20.00	10.35
20.45	11.05
	to
	20.05
	every 20 mins
	20.25 (A)
	20.45 (A,C)
	21.00 (A)
	21.20 (A)
	21.40 (A,C)
	21.50
	22.00 (C)
	22.30
	23.30

(A) To and from Los Cristianos
(B) To and from Playa de las Américas
(C) Service only runs on working days
(D) Sat and Sun only, as far as Los Cristianos

480

ARONA - LOS CRISTIANOS
Arona - La Sabinita - La Camella - Chayofa - **Los Cristianos**

ARONA		LOS CRISTIANOS
05.45		06.00
06.55	(A)	08.00
08.30		09.00
09.30		10.00
10.30		11.00
12.30		13.05
13.30		14.00
14.30		15.00
15.30		16.00
16.30		17.00
18.40		19.05
19.30		20.00
20.30		21.00

(A) Continues to Playa de las Américas

482

VILAFLOR - LOS CRISTIANOS
Vilaflor - **La Escalona** - **Arona** - La Sabinita - La Camella - Chayofa - **Los Cristianos**

VILAFLOR		LOS CRISTIANOS
06.35	(A)	06.00
12.00		11.00
18.15		17.00

(A) Continues to Playa de las Américas

LA GUAGUA DE ADEJE
Town service runs from 7.30 to 21.00, Mondays to Fridays only. Operates in a figure of eight west-east around the town, every 20-25 minutes.

GLOSSARY

This glossary contains Spanish and Canarian words used in the text (shown in *italics* in this book), plus other local words that you may encounter.

A

abandonado — abandoned, in poor repair
abierto — open
acampamiento — camping
acantilado — cliff
acequia — water channel
agua — water
agua no potable — water (not drinkable)
agua potable — drinking water
alto — high
aparcamiento — parking
arroyo — stream
autopista — main road, motorway
ayuntamiento — town hall

B

bajo — low
barranco — ravine
bocadillo — bread roll
bodegón — inn
bosque — wood

C

cabezo — peak, summit
cabra — goat
cabrera — goatherd
caldera — collapsed volcanic cone
calima — hot sand/dust laden wind
calle — street
camino — trail, path, track
camino particular — private road
camino real — old donkey trail (lit. royal road)
camino rural — single track tarmacked road
carretera — main road
casa — house
casa rural — country house accommodation

cascada — waterfall
caserío — hamlet, village
cementario — cemetery
cerrado — closed
cerveza — beer
dos cerveza — one beer, and another one
choza — shelter
clinica — clinic, hospital
colmena — bee hive
comida — food
cordillera — mountain range
correos — post office
cortijo — farmstead
costa — coast
coto privado de caza — private hunting area
Cruz Roja — Red Cross (medical aid)
cuesta — slope
cueva — cave
cumbre — summit

D

degollado — pass
derecha — right (direction)
desprendimiento — landslide

E

embalse — reservoir
ermita — chapel
Espacio Naturaleza Protegido — protected area of natural beauty, 'pa'
estación de autobus — bus station

F

farmacia — chemist
faro — lighthouse
fiesta — holiday, celebration
finca — farm, country house
fuente — spring

G

gasolinera	petrol station
guagua	bus
Guardia Civil	police
guia	guide

H

hostal	hostel, accommodation
hoya	depression (geological)

I

iglesia	church
información	information
isla	island
izquierda	left (direction)

L

lago	lake
lavadero	laundry area (usually communal)
librería	bookshop
llano	plain
lluvioso	rainy
lomo	broad-backed ridge

M

malpais	'bad lands' wild, barren countryside
mapa	map
mercado	market
mirador	lookout/viewing point
montaña	mountain

N

nublado	cloudy

O

oficina de turismo	tourist office

P

pa	protected area of natural beauty
parapente	hang-glider
peligroso	danger
pensión	guesthouse
pico	peak
picon	black volcanic rock/sand
pista	dirt road/track
pista (forestal)	forest road/track
playa	beach
plaza	square
policia	police
pozo	well

prohibido el paso	no entry
puente	bridge
puerto	port, mountain pass

R

refugio	refuge, shelter
río	river, stream
roque	rock
ruta	route

S

salida	exit
senda	path, track
sendero	foot path
sierra	mountain range
sin salida	no through road/route
sirocco	hot dust/sand laden wind

T

tapas	bar snacks
tienda	shop
tipico	traditional bar/eating place
tormentoso	stormy
torre	tower
torrente	stream
tubería	water pipe

V

valle	valley
vega	meadow
ventoso	windy
volcán	volcano

Z

zona recreativa	recreation area

DISCOVERY WALKING GUIDES

34 WALKS

- a series of Walking Guide Books

We receive praise for our regional walking guide titles in almost every post. Thanks to the many happy users of these guides, DWG has acquired an enviable reputation for interesting and accurately described, walking routes. Now the time is right for our new **34 Walks** series of walking guide books. These new books are wider ranging than our previous guides, covering whole islands or regions. All the routes have been newly researched and even our 'classic' routes have been re-walked and rewritten to ensure that they are up-to-date.

Each title in the **34 Walks** series is designed to provide a wide range of interesting routes for moderately fit walkers, plus some routes for experienced walkers. Thanks to the feedback we receive from walkers we have designed these books so that you have the best walking guide book for the destination. Features in **34 Walks** books include:-

- walking route summary
- fully detailed walk descriptions including frequent timings
- GPS Waypoints (grid references) for all key points on a route
- detailed map at 1:25,000 or 1:40,000 scale for every walking route
- full GPS Waypoint lists for all the walking routes

Add in useful background information, and you have the best value walking guides that you can buy.

34 Walks books form one part of DWG's complete walking package. For each title there is also a **Tour & Trail Map**, or **Walkers' Maps** to complement each book.

Available from good book shops or by mail order. For up to date information on Discovery Walking Guides publications write to DWG Ltd, 10 Tennyson Close, Northampton NN5 7HJ, England or visit:-
www.walking.demon.co.uk or
www.dwgwalking.co.uk

DISCOVERY WALKING GUIDES

TRAIL & TRAIL 1:40,000 SCALE MAPS

Tour & Trail Maps were developed to meet the needs for accurate and up-to-date maps for destinations covered by Discovery Walking Guides. At the core of each **T&T** map design is a comprehensive ground-level survey carried out by car and on foot. The survey results are then translated into DWG's design programme, to produce a digital vector graphic database involving the organisation of several million pieces of information across a large number of 'layers' drawn digitally within our computers. Once a DWG digital vector graphic database has been established, new developments such as new roads and tracks, can be quickly incorporated into the correct layer of the database. Rapid updating, combined with state of the art 'file to plate' pre-press operation, enables DWG to produce new editions of **Tour & Trail Maps** quickly and efficiently.

Tour & Trail Maps have a Latitude/Longitude grid and datum information making them GPS compatible. DWG walking routes are clearly highlighted on **T&T** maps, along with their GPS Waypoints wherever space allows.

From 2003, all new **Tour & Trail Maps** titles will be produced on a super-durable material which is waterproof and tear-proof, making **T&T** maps the toughest maps available, in addition to being the most accurate and up-to-date.

Tour & Trail Maps are available for:-

- **Alpujarras**

- **Madeira**

- **La Gomera**

- **Gran Canaria Mountains**

- **Mallorca North & Mountains**

- **Menorca**

New to accompany our **34 Walks** series of guide books is a series of **Walkers' Maps** at a 1:25,000 scale, 4cms = 1km, a scale that is so popular for UK walking.

The interesting walking regions for destinations such as Lanzarote and Tenerife form pockets around the island, and a whole island **Tour & Trail Map** would not be viable; Tenerife at 1:40,000 scale would make a 3 metres by 2 metres map and Lanzarote would only be a bit smaller. Just try unfolding something that size while out on a walking route!

To solve the problem of providing top quality mapping at a pocketable size, we have developed **Walkers' Maps** which bring together the walking regions at 1:25,000 scale onto a single folded map at a size to fit your pocket. This gives you large scale maps for all the routes in a **34 Walks** guide book in one map product.

Tenerife Walkers' Maps will consist of 1:25,000 map sections covering routes in the South (4 map sections), West (one large map section), Las Cañadas/Teide (3 map sections) and the North (one large map section) plus an island locator map. The full **Tenerife Walkers' Map** and **Lanzarote Walkers' Map** are published in two editions; a low cost Paper edition and a Super-Durable waterproof and tearproof edition, using the same materials and techniques as for **Indestructible Maps**.

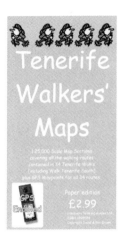

Drive! Touring Maps are designed for today's drivers with the emphasis on accuracy and clarity. Using the digital vector graphic databases from our **Tour & Trail Maps**, plus specially commissioned surveys, **Drive! Touring Maps** are completely up to date on publication. Being up to date is important as Spain has recently changed its road numbering system, which makes driving very confusing if using an old map.

Special design criteria have been developed which result in exceptional clarity, while emphasising the motorist's needs for quick recognition of junctions, road numbers, petrol stations and refreshment stops with off-road parking.

Each **Drive! Touring Map** includes:-
- a comprehensive Place Name Index
- a Distance Chart for main destinations
- datum and grid information enabling the map to be used with modern GPS equipment

All this is backed up by:-
- large scale Street Plans which include Place Names Indexes for major resorts

Drive! Touring Maps include everything you need for exploring these exciting destinations by car.

Drive Touring Maps are available, or in development (D) for:-

- **Tenerife**

- **Lanzarote**

- **La Gomera** (D)

- **Gran Canaria** (D)

- **Fuerteventura** (D)

- **La Palma** (D)

- **Madeira**

- **Mallorca** (D)

- **Menorca**

DISCOVERY WALKING GUIDES

PERSONAL NAVIGATOR FILES

Getting lost is not a pleasant experience, while getting lost in a foreign destination can be distinctly unpleasant. DWG have an excellent reputation for accurately researched and described walking routes, but even we can go further with our revolutionary **Personal Navigator Files**.

All DWG's **34 Walks** series of books are researched using modern GPS equipment, giving us an accuracy of better than five metres. GPS gives us extremely accurate walking routes, and DWG knows exactly where our authors have walked. Now we are making this GPS Track and Waypoint information available for GPS users in a range of formats to suit popular GPS software such as Oziexplorer, GPSY, Fuginawa.

If you have a GPS, download lead and GPS software for your PC, then DWG's new **Personal Navigator Files** will mean that you can follow in the exact footsteps of our walking authors; now that really is 'vorsprung technik' for walkers.

Personal Navigator Files are available for:-

● **Alpujarras**

● **Tenerife**

● **Lanzarote**

- and will be available for all new **34 Walks** destinations. For more information, see DWG websites:-

www.walking.demon.co.uk
and
www.dwgwalking.co.uk

We've all suffered from maps that fall apart, split down the folds, and soak up water like a sponge. Sellotape, or better drafting tape, is pressed into service to repair the ailing paper map to try and make it last a bit longer. At DWG we believe in durability but even we admit that our paper maps have a limited life when subjected to the rigours of outdoors adventuring. So putting our money where our mouth is, we have formed **The Indestructible Map Company Ltd (TIMCo)**, which does exactly what it says in the name; it produces **Indestructible Maps** which are 'Guaranteed for Life'.

TIMCo combines DWG's expertise in researching and designing the best maps, with the latest materials technology and printing techniques, to produce the I**ndestructible Map**. They tell us that the material is a 'high density polymer' core to which they fuse a printable layer of a China Clay type compound; well, they lost us somewhere around 'density' but we do know that what we have got is a map that in 'normal' use will last you a lifetime. It is waterproof, tear-proof, and just about proof to everything apart from fire and attack with sharp objects. You can fold it into a rain hat or beer glass - we've tried, so we know it works - and then still use it as the best map. It feels like silk but appears to have the strength of carbon fibre. You get all of these attributes in an **Indestructible Map** and all at a ridiculous price of £4.99.

Indestructible Maps are not easy to produce - otherwise all map publishers would be using these materials and techniques. Paper is easy. It has been around for hundreds of years and printing paper has been highly developed, plus paper is cheap. Specially coated high density polymer is expensive, eye-wateringly expensive. Printers don't like polymers; they have to run their machines more slowly (more expense), use special inks (very expensive) and put special dryers between each stage of the printing process.

On the first print run of **Tenerife Indestructible Map** our printers forgot some of the complex settings and 455 copies of **Tenerife Indestructible Map** fused themselves into a solid indestructible lump; unfortunately the printers dumped the mistake or we might have been short-listed for the Turner prize!

After all this, you have a lovely **Indestructible Map** as a flat sheet, but that is not the end of your problems. Folding an Indestructible material is a real problem as it always remembers that it once was a flat sheet; TIMCo have to keep the boxes of printed maps sealed until use otherwise we have a lot of flat maps which were once folded!

Enough of the moans and whinges about producing **Indestructible Maps** - just try one for yourself. We are convinced that TIMCo is the future of maps, and we will be using these materials and techniques for DWG's new **Tour & Trail Maps** and **Walkers' Maps**.

www.indestructiblemap.co.uk

WALKING IN THE CANARY ISLANDS

TENERIFE

Despite its 'tabloid' image Tenerife has some of the best walking routes and is suitable for a wide range of walking abilities, up to the most experienced mountain walkers. Once away from the tourist resorts and urban areas, walkers are rewarded with an extensive network of trails and *pistas* on which to explore the unspoilt landscapes. High altitude walking - 2,200 to 3,700 metres altitude - is available in the Las Cañadas/Mount Teide national park. The south and west of the island offer spectacular walking routes combined with easy access from the resorts, as does the upper Orotava Valley in the north. Further afield, the isolated Anaga peninsula will reward walkers prepared to make the long drive from the resorts.

Publications available :-
- **34 Tenerife Walks**
- **Walk Tenerife South**
- **Tenerife Walkers' Maps**
- **Tenerife Indestructible Map**
- **Drive! Tenerife Touring Map**

LA GOMERA

This national heritage island is a walking paradise with spectacular routes in all regions of La Gomera. Garajonay laurel forest is at the island's heart surrounded by huge *barrancos* offering walkers some of the best walking routes in the Canary Islands. Valle Gran Rey and Playa Santiago are developing as resorts but the rest of the island has been blissfully overlooked and offers the rural idyll many seek, if you are prepared for the laborious journey of a flight to Tenerife, transfer to Los Cristianos for ferry to La Gomera; best to book for two weeks or more to make the most of your time on our favourite island.

Publications available :-
- **34 La Gomera Walks**
- **La Gomera Tour & Trail Map**
- **Drive! La Gomera Touring Map**

LA PALMA

Spectacular La Palma is becoming better known, thanks to direct flights from Manchester and Gatwick, plus recent TV programmes. The world's steepest island rises direct from the sea to the high *cumbre* which forms the rim of the Taburiente. The island government has recently installed new waymarking posts and signs covering a wide range of routes. Very rewarding walking for the fitter walker.

LANZAROTE

The fire island is becoming more popular with leisure walkers. Despite having nothing over 700 metres in height, the desert and volcanic landscape contains a surprising variety of walking experiences. Escape from the intensively developed resorts and you will discover landscapes of a barren grandeur, plus a surprising variety of endemic plant life.

Publications available :-
- **34 Lanzarote Walks**
- **Lanzarote Walkers' Maps**
- **Lanzarote Indestructible Map**
- **Drive! Lanzarote Touring Map**

GRAN CANARIA

The best walking is some distance from the southern resorts, centred around Roque Nublo in the centre of the island and stretching westwards. Tremendous scenery amongst the massive canyons combines with a good network of trails to reward adventurous walkers.

Publications available :-
- **Gran Canaria Mountains Tour & Trail Map**
- **Gran Canaria Indestructible Map**
- **Drive Gran Canaria Touring Map**

EL HIERRO

The smallest and least known Canary Island has some of the most varied landscapes of any of the seven islands. Known to ancient mariners as the edge of the known world, it was once the home of the International Meridian which can still be seen on the western tip, before its move to Greenwich. Tiresome plane and ferry transfers mean that El Hierro has been overlooked by mass tourism, giving the island a Shangri-La quality for whose seeking peace and tranquillity. Interesting walking among varied landscapes far from the tourism crowds.

FUERTEVENTURA

'Strong Wind Island' is famous for its huge beaches, windsurfing and naturism. Most barren of the Canary Islands, there is little life outside of the resorts and island capital of Puerto Rosario. A few reasonable walking routes but generally this is an island more suited to Jeep Safari than walking.

Publications available :-
- **Fuerteventura Indestructible Map**
- **Drive! Fuerteventura Touring Map**

USEFUL PHONE NUMBERS
& ADDRESSES

N.B.
All Tenerife numbers are prefixed by **922**, with the exception of the emergency numbers.

When dialling from outside Spain, prefix the number with **00 34**

Emergencies	
(pan-European number)	
Fire, police, ambulance, civil defence	**112**
Policia Nacional	**091**
Policia Local	**092**
Guardia Civil	**062**
Urgencias Salud	**061**
(medical emergencies)	

Taxis	
Adeje area	**922 741612**
Arona area	**922 790352**
Los Cristianos	**922 796611**
Playa de las Américas	**922 714468**

There are plenty of taxis in the larger towns. Most villages have a public telephone, and some bars have a pay phone. Bar owners will usually phone for a taxi on your behalf, but buy a drink too.

Tourist Information Offices

UK
Oficina Española de Turismo
22-23 Manchester Square
London W1M 5AP
020 7486 8077

www.tourspain.es
londres@tourspain.es

TENERIFE
Oficina De Turismo Cabildo
Insular
Plaza España
E-38003   **922 60 58 00**
S. C. de Tenerife   **922 23 95 92**

Oficina De Turismo
General Franco
Los Cristianos   **922 75 71 37**

Oficina De Turismo
Av. Rafael Puig Lluvina 1
Costa Adeje   **922 75 06 33**

There are also Tourism Offices at the beaches of Playa Fañabe, Playas Troya, and Playa las Vistas. For exact locations, see the Playa de las Américas/Los Cristianos street plan on either the **Drive! Tenerife Touring Map** or **Tenerife Indestructible Map**.